Who Are All These

CHILDREN

and Why Are They Calling Me

M♥M?

Embracing the Joyful Mess
of Motherhood

Who Are All These
CHILDREN
and Why Are They Calling Me
M♥M?

Embracing the Joyful Mess
of Motherhood

**FAITH
BOGDAN**

CHARISMA HOUSE

Most CHARISMA HOUSE BOOK GROUP products are available at special quantity discounts for bulk purchase for sales promotions, premiums, fund-raising, and educational needs. For details, write Charisma House Book Group, 600 Rinehart Road, Lake Mary, Florida 32746, or telephone (407) 333-0600.

WHO ARE ALL THESE CHILDREN AND WHY ARE THEY CALLING ME MOM? by Faith Bogdan
Published by Charisma House
Charisma Media/Charisma House Book Group
600 Rinehart Road, Lake Mary, Florida 32746
www.charismahouse.com

Unless otherwise noted, all Scripture quotations are from the Holy Bible, New International Version. Copyright © 1973, 1978, 1984, International Bible Society. Used by permission.

Scripture quotations marked ASV are from the American Standard Bible. Public domain.

Scripture quotations marked BBE are from the Bible in Basic English. Public domain.

Scripture quotations marked DARBY are from the Darby Translation of the Bible. Public domain.

Scripture quotations marked ESV are from the Holy Bible, English Standard Version. Copyright © 2001 by Crossway Bibles, a division of Good News Publishers. Used by permission.

Scripture quotations marked ISV are taken from the Holy Bible: International Standard Version. Copyright © 1996–2012 by The ISV Foundation. All rights reserved internationally. Used by permission.

Scripture quotations marked KJV are from the King James Version of the Bible. Public domain.

Scripture quotations marked NAS are from the New American Standard Bible. Copyright © 1960, 1962, 1963, 1968, 1971, 1972, 1973, 1975, 1977 by the Lockman Foundation. Used by permission. (www.Lockman.org)

Cover design by Nancy Panaccione
Design Director: Bill Johnson

AUTHOR'S NOTE: Some names, places, and identifying details with regard to stories in this book have been changed to help protect the privacy of individuals.

Visit the author's website at www.faithbogdan.com.

Library of Congress Cataloging-in-Publication Data:
An application to register this book for cataloging has been submitted to the Library of Congress.
International Standard Book Number: 978-1-62136-028-5
E-book ISBN: 978-1-62136-029-2

While the author has made every effort to provide accurate telephone numbers and Internet addresses at the time of publication, neither the publisher nor the author assumes any responsibility for errors or for changes that occur after publication.

First edition

13 14 15 16 17 — 9 8 7 6 5 4 3 2 1
Printed in the United States of America

To my husband and best friend, Dave.

☙

*This book would not have been possible
without you. I mean, after all…*

Contents

Introduction

IS IT JUST ME?

Psst—over here! I'm hiding out in the laundry room, eating dark chocolate. Got a sec? Good. I was wondering, is it just me, or do you sometimes find it *really hard* to be a mom? Even after all the parenting books you've read, do you still fear that one more sibling squabble is going to send you running down the street like a madwoman? Do you dream of a candlelit bath in a tub that isn't brimming with slimy grow-in-water toys and all the towels you just washed? Do you miss date nights, hot meals—or just *meals*? Have you forgotten what "quiet" sounds like, what peace feels like? Do you barely remember what you looked like before dark bags inflated under your eyes? You don't need another manual on motherhood—you need an eighteen-year chill pill.

Moments of mothering disillusionment happen to the best of us. We sigh over unused potential or shelved talents and wonder if we'll *ever* get past diapering to see our dreams fulfilled. Even as we relish being a mom and adore our little munchkins to pieces, there are too many of *those days*—when we're bone-tired and the baby is sick, Diego has wet his pants for the fourth time, and Emma wants to be read to *again*.

At times like these we don't exactly feel passionately in

love with this child-rearing career. When Emma plops into your lap with a worn-out copy of *Green Eggs and Ham*, you want to kiss her on the cheek and snuggle up for a good read like you want to scarf down her uneaten bowl of cold brussels sprouts.

Then there are those of us who go beyond just having our "moments." Underneath the day-to-day motions we go through, we bear a quiet disappointment with our lot in life. We harbor secret resentment about the way our kids constantly interrupt our plans, our conversations, and our sleep. From time to time these attitudes leak (or gush) out and reveal themselves to our children—in the sharpness of our tone, the looks we shoot their way, and even in what we *don't* do or say.

I understand these feelings as well as anyone; I'm an "accidental mom"—a would-be career woman. I cried over a positive pregnancy test—and not with tears of joy. I know what it is to watch a doting mom in the park with a baby on her hip and five little ones trailing behind her and scratch my head in bewilderment. I confess to having looked at my "little blessings" and asking myself, "What did we *do?*"

If you have ever been tempted to daydream for a second about how much easier life would be with one or two fewer children, if you have bemoaned the "good ole days" of childless, mess-less bliss, if you ever looked at a faint pink line in the window of a pregnancy test and said, "Oops," "*Again?*", "God help me," or "*Nooooo!*"—this book is for you. And yet it's not just for you. I also write to those who always dreamed of being a mom and yet struggle through long days. You may not rant and rave in high decibels over your kid's spilled milk, but mothering still scores low on the job satisfaction scale. You've lost your joy for the journey—or perhaps you think true and constant enjoyment of motherhood is something for mothers of a different era, culture, or species.

I know motherhood can be difficult—and it doesn't always knock before entering a life. Perhaps you were a carefree newlywed who cried over a positive pregnancy test or a pregnant teenager who decided to keep her baby. Maybe you recently discovered a "last-minute family surprise" is on the way and you just turned forty-two. Perhaps you're a grandmother who surrendered your tidy empty nest to raise rowdy grandchildren.

Or maybe that "rhythm method" wasn't all it was cracked out to be, and you ended up with a fuller "quiver" than you bargained for. Perhaps you wanted—even planned—all the children you have, and you simply want to fall in love with them to the fullest degree. No matter how you became a mom or what your experience has been like so far, this book is for you.

It is not merely a discourse on the importance of healthy child-rearing. Neither is it another how-to on being a great mother. I believe a woman can understand and appreciate the value of motherhood, and even be good at parenting, but not have a tender heart for her children. I should know.

This is my story of journeying from where I used to be— an embittered, detached mother living in survival mode— to where I am today: a mom who is madly in love with the children she didn't intend to have. I will take you to the places in my heart I once dared not let anyone see—to my questions about God and conception, guilt over those questions, and feelings of total failure as a mother. I hope that by the end of my story you'll agree that if I can end up wildly surprised by the thrill of having "all these children," so can you.

Loving Life With Kids

I've had a recurring nightmare at least a couple times a year since becoming a mom. I dream that I get to the end of a day, or two days or three, and realize I've forgotten to nurse my baby. In fact, I don't even know where my baby is. I frantically search for her, wondering if she's dehydrated or still alive. I always wake up before finding out what happens next.

Relief washes over me, and at the same time, shame and regret—regret that I have valued my life, my plans, my time, my to-do lists above my babies. I am trying to rid myself of those nightmares. I could have written these pages in half the years it took me—and failed to nurture my babies in the process.

After writing half of this book, I put it on the shelf for a few years in order to live it. When I returned to my unfinished manuscript, I was shocked at how things had changed. Not only were my children older and life was easier, but also I had fallen in love with the children who fell into my lap. Motherhood was no longer about surviving or even being a "good mom." It was about a very imperfect mother loving life with kids.

If you'd like to find or rediscover that place, I'd like to point you in that direction. I don't pretend to know all the answers, but I'll share the joys and sorrows along my own journey that helped to bring me to where I am today. I'll even share some of the practical wisdom I've gained through fifteen years of learning from my mistakes and successes and through observing other moms. We'll discuss things like discipline, the marriage relationship, adult friendships, family devotions, fun-time activities, and self-discovery. I have by no means arrived at perfection, but now I have hope for becoming the mother my children need and discovering the purpose for this life I once held in disdain.

I have interviewed countless mothers, some of whom, like me, didn't always relish the idea of being called "Mommy." They come from all walks of life, and each has her own set of unique circumstances. These are everyday women: your neighbor, your boss, the quiet woman in your moms' group, the lady at Costco hovering over a screaming toddler, or that girl who recently visited your church. You may even see your own face reflected in the honest words of the women who helped me write these pages.

I know you're nonstop busy. Feel free to set this book in that pretty basket in your bathroom (hey, isn't that the only place where you can read?) and meditate on small portions of it in those precious minutes alone. I've made it easy to carry nuggets of truth with you throughout the day in the form of one-line *Refrigerator Magnets*. There are also *Heart Exams* at the end of each chapter—probing questions about motherhood that no one may have asked you before. Journal your responses, and then come back to them in a few years. I hope you'll be as pleasantly surprised as I was to find out how much you've grown in love for your children and for yourself as a mother.

No matter how or why you started out as a parent, if you need encouragement for the days ahead and new-found passion for your kids, read on. I hope that by the time you reach the end of this book you'll be able to say, even on your worst days, "I love being a mom!"

 Refrigerator Magnet: Love is not a feeling— it is a choice.

Heart Exam: Why am I reading this book?

Chapter 1

OOPS, I'M A MOM!

To the unknowing eye it might seem that Dave and I had this parenthood thing all planned from the beginning. We both came from happy, four-children, two-parent, churchgoing homes. I'm a homeschooling nut who actually looks forward to Mondays. Dave is one of those rare "Mr. Wonderfuls" who changes soupy, up-the-back, newborn diapers at 3:00 a.m. and bathes squirming toddlers before giving them elephant rides to bed. We are the couple who should have naturally wanted to have children.

But nineteen years ago, while on a dinner date, Dave and I observed a young family at a nearby table. The parents were attempting to converse over filet mignon with their three-year-old present. When the child's milk-soaked paper menu was no longer colorable, he turned his attention to splattering ketchup, making mac-and-cheese sculptures, and whining incessantly for dessert.

After the frustrated mother wiped the child's cheesy face (against his ear-splitting objections) and hurried out of the restaurant, I asked Dave, "So, do you want to have children?"

"Not really." He smiled tentatively.

"Perfect!" I thought. We got married seven months later.

Childless Bliss

OK, our decision to marry was based on a little more than our mutual desire to remain childless. But one thing was clear in both our minds: we were happy and carefree, and if we could help it, children were not going to ruin that.

My Friday morning phone conversations with friends sounded something like this: "Hi, Melissa! You guys doin' anything tonight? Wanna go out? Oh wait, I forgot; you have *children*."

Then Dave and I would elbow each other with a sarcastic, "Don't you want to have two or three kids?" We'd spend the rest of the day doing...you know, for the life of me, I can't remember what on earth we did with our time!

I do remember one thing: we prayed together. Surrounded by the cornfields of tiny Barton in rural upstate New York, we knelt habitually by the couch in our singlewide trailer and pled with God to ultimately have His way concerning the planning of our family. We didn't want kids, but we did want God's will for our lives. If it included children, we wanted to be open to that. So we always prayed that, God willing, He would overrule any measures we took that would botch His plan for us. Neither of us wanted to wake up one day in our fifties and realize, sadly, that it was too late to have a family.

To this day I do not fully understand our past desire to remain childless. I have no idea whether we would have ever "woken up to smell a family." I'm as clueless as the people who ask incredulously, "How could you not want kids?" When I see a childless couple, I imagine they are unable to have children or that they've devoted their lives to taking care of animals and the planet. They're the couple who shares a bed with a pot-bellied pig and names house plants, going through a grieving process when the ferns shrivel up and die. None of that was the case with Dave and me; we were just plain selfish, I guess.

We spent the first three years of our married life in childless bliss. I contemplated furthering my education, setting my sights on a PhD. The possibilities were endless: I imagined traveling the world as a journalist or becoming a snarky syndicated columnist...editing *Newsweek* magazine or prosecuting dangerous criminals in high courts of law. I'd love to write that I had to leave a six-figure salary to stay at home and wash burp cloths: "Yes, Oprah, it was quite the switch, going from Wall Street to fixing up a nursery."

Not that I bought into the notion that I could be anything I wanted to be. But I like to dream, and firstborn self-confidence got the best of me. I once over-sold myself in a job interview as a data entry clerk who could process Swedish specs for the design of high-speed trains. Then later I talked my way into a job as a cocktail waitress. I didn't know a lick of Swedish, hardly had a left brain, and couldn't tell a martini from a Coke. I got fired from both jobs. Even while doing a college stint as a front-end cashier at McDonald's, I once accidentally greeted an early-morning customer with, "Hi, may I hold you?" Looking back, it appears I was never meant to work outside the home.

So there was no dramatic switch in career paths. It wasn't all that difficult to say good-bye to my low-paying position as a job placement specialist (aka "job coach") for people with learning disabilities. Nevertheless, I felt that getting pregnant would forever destroy my hopes of climbing the ladder of success.

Success to me wasn't a yacht and vacation house in Maui. When I wasn't working or dreaming of being famous, I practiced the piano, scoured wealthy neighborhoods for garage-sale treasures, decorated our trailer with I-beat-the-antique-dealers finds, and shopped the mall till I dropped.

On the weekends Dave and I took long country walks, went out to dinner, and slept in late. We enjoyed occasional getaways in honeymoon resorts or in our two-man tent among the majestic trees and quiet lakes of upper New York's Adirondacks. We did it all child free, carefree, hopelessly in love, and supremely happy.

"Fire Baby"

Wanting to make our rent money count for something, we bought a HUD property—a small, pink, fixer-upper farmhouse foreclosure in nearby Erin, New York. Everything needed to be redone except the foundation. But I saw potential in that little two-bedroom structure. We envisioned it becoming like something on the cover of *Country Home*, and I dreamed of spending my days off making crafts or canning peaches if I ever felt so inclined. The spare bedroom would double as my writing room and a place to store Dave's hunting toys. It would be the perfect home for a DINK couple ("Double Income–No Kids").

Dave spent a year renovating the house on the weekends with the help of a few dedicated friends. In April of 1996 we boxed up the contents of our trailer, eager to move into our first home. But a week before I was to be carried over the threshold, our handyman special burned to the ground.

Dave took me to the Best Western that night to console me. He must have really comforted me well, because a few weeks later I experienced flu-like symptoms. Several days after that I was confronted with the life-changing verdict of a pregnancy test. The memories of asking God to be our family planner were washed away with tears of anguish.

I'll never forget sitting in the doctor's office awaiting the results of my blood work, convinced that discount-store home pregnancy kits are defective and untrustworthy. A cheerful, middle-aged doctor came in and asked how I was feeling.

"I think I might be pregnant," I murmured.

"Well, you are!" her voice sing-songed through the room. She was thrilled to be the bearer of "good news."

Everything seemed to go dark, and the doctor sounded far away as she continued to talk. I felt a strange mixture of horror and joy. I didn't know whether to laugh or cry.

Needing to tell someone, I sped to my friend Cynthia's house and rapped on her door. She opened it and stood there, one hand on a vacuum cleaner, the other hand on a swollen belly. This was her fourth pregnancy, and, still plagued by morning sickness, she was the misery that likes company.

"I've decided to join you," I announced.

"What do you mean?" she asked. "You're going to help me clean house?"

"No-o-o-o," I grinned sheepishly. "When you found out

you were pregnant, you asked me if I wanted to join you. Well...I did!" I was just as shocked to hear myself say those words as she was. We cried and hugged each other.

After surviving three months of eating every salty, starchy, doughy thing I could get my hands on, I felt better about having our "fire baby." I even began to get a little excited. I decided that if I had to have a child, I could at least hope for a boy. A girl was out of the question. I had put a lot of gray hairs on my mother's head with my female antics and smart-mouth attitude. You reap what you sow, and I didn't want any seeds of sassiness coming back to bite me.

Besides, I thought girls were whiney, catty, and high-maintenance in every area—from hair grooming to conflicts over who gets to play with the blonde Barbie. Boys, on the other hand, were emotionally stable and looked adorable in cowboy boots and holsters. And it would be only right for God to give my outdoorsy husband a son to accompany him on big game hunting trips and fishing expeditions in Alaska. With each shopping trip I ventured into the baby department and fingered blue outfits, picturing denim and flannel on our little "Benjamin David."

With our homeowner's insurance money we purchased a log home in the woods just south of the New York state border in Gillett, Pennsylvania—one with a third bedroom to accommodate houseguests. I prepared a blue-and-green Noah's Ark nursery.

On New Year's Eve in 1996 Dave and I were watching a movie appropriately titled *Independence Day* at the home of our friends Cliff and Nina Horton. At four o'clock in the morning I went upstairs and tried to sleep, but a half-hour later I began feeling recurring little cramps in my belly. I timed them: they were five faithful minutes apart. I waddled back down the stairs, planted myself in front of the movie, and asked, "What are contractions like?" As Nina described what I was feeling, I sat down and felt my water break—right on her tapestry couch.

It appeared, Nina said, I was in labor, two weeks before my due date. I was not happy about this for two reasons: one, I was not ready. I had not "nested," as they say a mother is instinctively supposed to do right before delivery. I hadn't dusted the light fixtures, canned beans, or ironed a month's worth of underwear. Since this was my first baby, I counted on being overdue. People seemed to think that all first babies came late. That was fine with me.

Secondly, I had been up all night celebrating the New Year. We played War, gorged ourselves on shrimp cocktail and crackers, and watched that movie. It was bad enough a baby had interrupted my life; I felt he could have at least had the courtesy to let me sleep in on the holiday.

But there I was, in flat-out denial, standing before the nurse's station at Robert Packer Hospital early on New Year's Day. Water trickled down my legs, soaking my sweatpants, and I declared repeatedly, "I am *not* in labor!" I begged Dave to take me home to sleep. He suppressed a smile that made me want to kick him. We sent a friend to our house a half-hour away to pack up my nightclothes and bring them to the hospital. I felt God was playing a mean trick on me.

That evening, after being hooked up to a beguiling Pitocin drip, I finally experienced heavy labor. After two hours of off-the-chart contractions, I screamed for the epidural I'd valiantly refused all day. Dave cried, seeing my pain. "Too late," my midwife said, "You're a ten!" Roaring like a primitive tribeswoman passing a pumpkin, I gave birth to Anna Grace.

She was, astonishingly, a girl.

The following morning I phoned my supervisor over a hospital tray of scrambled eggs and sausage links. "Mr. Freeman," I said, my voice quivering, "This is Faith—the chick you hired only months ago in hopes of enhancing the Exceptional Education program. It, uh, seems I've had a baby. I won't be returning to work."

 Refrigerator Magnet: We can chart our own course, but God is the one who guides the ship (Prov. 16:9).

 Heart Exam: What part of my life do I need to hold with an open hand?

Chapter 2

WHO ARE ALL THESE CHILDREN?

DAVE AND I brought Anna home in a green sleeper, and I sat in my rustic living room, rocking her and thinking, "Now what?" As I nursed her in the dusky shadows of nightfall, a sense of foreboding, a feeling that life would never be the same, crept over me. My emotions were a confused muddle of self-pity and elation over the little body I held in my arms. It seemed my fast-track life had come to a screeching halt, and I was stuck in the darkness like a broken-down car on an amusement park ride.

Should I wait to see if life-my-way would resume? Or should I face reality and get off and walk, baby in arms, to find some new and slower track to go on? What I really wanted to do was curl up and cry. I felt my hope of another college degree, a job promotion, a published book, travels, and the like were all gone. I was suddenly the prisoner of an infant's dependence, and there was no turning back.

Rude Awakening

The first discovery I made as a mother was in keeping with what all new moms say: "I never realized how selfish I was!" For example, I had been accustomed to a weekly "night out on the town," which included shopping until my wallet was empty and my eyes were red with fatigue. I joked about having ongoing affairs with "the three other men in my life": Michaels, TJ Maxx, and Peter Harris.

And little Anna, sweet as she was, was not going to interfere with those shopping affairs. So on one such evening when I needed a mall fix, I left her at home with Dave and headed out the door. I wasn't going to let a newborn hinder my money-spending mission. Pushing a stroller—not to mention stopping for nursing sessions— would have most definitely put a damper on my "night out with me."

Hours later I headed home with three cents left and a pair of shoes in every color weighing me down. From the driveway I could hear the siren of a starving newborn going off. I raced through the front door and met a man pacing back and forth like an angry grizzly bear, swinging a screaming infant through the air to no avail. No words were exchanged as I quickly nursed Anna back to health. The glare in Dave's eyes assured me that I'd be accompanied by a very young chaperone on my next shopping date. But that wasn't enough to keep me out of retail therapy. I soon learned that dressing rooms make great places to observe oneself from various angles even when you're breast-feeding.

Eventually I settled comfortably into mommy mode

and began to enjoy having just one child. Anna was a pretty good first and last baby. I could already tell she had her daddy's even-keeled temperament. I'd always thought that no child should grow up without a sibling if it could be helped, but now the tables were turned. We'd buy Anna a puppy.

Not Again!

That summer I was grocery shopping one morning with seven-month-old Anna riding happily atop the cart. As I strolled through the meat department, I suddenly felt light-headed and nauseous. I recognized the mocking symptoms. *"Not again!"* I wailed inwardly. Sure enough, I'd come down with a bad case of pregnancy.

I went home and phoned a friend with my tragic news, hoping for comfort. "There's a way to prevent this kind of thing, you know," she laughed. I hung up on her. To this day, when a woman tells me she's pregnant, I consciously react as though she has won a trip to Bermuda. I don't care if she has nine kids already and is carrying triplets.

After Dave got home from work, I stood sobbing in his arms, staring at another positive pregnancy test, not seeing anything positive about it at all. Anna was still nursing and not yet sleeping through the night. I'd been tired enough *not* being pregnant. What on earth was I going to do? I unpacked my maternity clothes and resigned myself to my fate, figuring this time I'd at least get a boy.

"Miracle Baby"

Legend has it the women in my family are given to speedy labors and deliveries. Even my sister, Grace, once had a baby in the shower. She named her Glory Rain.

When I went into labor for the second time, Dave rushed me to the hospital after depositing baby Anna into her grandparents' arms. Grace, unmarried at the time, joined us in the delivery room, where the labor nurse pricked the "sac," and released a warm gush of water, followed by the appearance of a tuft of red hair.

"Is that the *head*?" Grace said.

But the nurse was too distracted to answer. "Dr. Williams! Dr. Williams!" she yelled down the hall. Sarah Hope was characteristically in a hurry to discover new worlds and would not be detained by a doctor stuck in an elevator somewhere. Out she whooshed from the birth canal and greeted the room with her mouth full of meconium. It got into her lungs.

I didn't know this until a couple hours later. Where was Sarah? Why hadn't they brought my baby back from her bathing, pricking, and weighing session? I buzzed the nurses' station. A pediatrician came and told me that Sarah had gone into respiratory distress and was facing the possibility of being airlifted to a neonatal unit.

My heart raced at the news. "God, please don't take my baby! Even if she is another girl!"

When the room cleared of people, I reached for the worn Bible I had packed and let it fall open. My eyes rested on Isaiah 51:12–13: "Who are you that you should be afraid of a man who will die... and you forget the LORD your Maker" (NKJV)?

"Lord," I wept, "help me not to be afraid of the doctor's report but to trust You to save my daughter!"

I spent the next nineteen hours by Sarah's side (except when I left to get a few hours of much-needed sleep). She lay in an observation tank, her purple chest heaving rapidly under a network of wires and electrode pads. Her chalky blue eyes watched me intently as I choked out a song against the beeping of monitors. Over and over I sang the words:

> Jesus loves you, this I know,
> For the Bible tells me so.
> Little ones to Him belong,
> They are weak, but He is strong!

I realized if God loved Sarah and she belonged to Him, surely He had her best interests at heart. No matter what, I could trust Him. Two days after her birth we brought Sarah home from the hospital, pink and healthy. She joined her "big sister" in the Noah's Ark room.

When that foreboding feeling surfaced again, I recognized it as postpartum blues. That knowledge made my emotions a little easier to deal with, though my hopes and dreams for a life beyond motherhood seemed to get buried deeper with the addition of each child to our family.

Monster Mom

Shortly after birth Sarah had been pumped full of antibiotics due to her respiratory trauma. The medication made her gassy. For the first several nights at home she woke up crying inconsolably every half hour. I quickly reached my wit's end. One night, after being jolted once again out of a deep sleep, I picked her up, looked at her, and cried, "Will you *please shut up*?" At that moment I was introduced to that familiar feeling moms love to hate: guilt.

The next few years were exhausting. Caring for two adventuresome preschoolers sapped me of all energy and patience. Sleep was a luxury I possessed only in my memory. I didn't handle things very well. Every night at eight o'clock I disappeared and a monster took my place. Monster Mom growled at little Sarah, ordering her to stay in bed and stop calling me back upstairs.

One night I heard a whimpering sound coming from beneath the blanket that covered my demanding daughter. "What's wrong *now*?" I barked.

"I don't wike it when you get upset," she cried.

A jolted Monster Mom was instantly replaced with a shame-filled mommy. I knelt at Sarah's bedside and held her tightly as tears of remorse dripped down to her golden locks. I began to pray for a change in myself, "And God, make it quick, while my kids are young enough to forget what I've been like."

Eventually I got my darlings potty trained and shed two years' worth of pregnancy weight. I dug my "skinny clothes" out of the attic and started lifting dumbbells. I now had kids—not babies—and I liked that. We were going places again—literally! Cabin fever was replaced with the ability to get my growing children out of the house and into the car faster than they could say, "I gotta go potty."

I determined never to get pregnant again.

Another "Positive"

Four years later I started wondering what it would be like to actually *want* to get pregnant. How would it feel to wake up one morning and realize I longed to hold a baby in my arms? I wondered how it would feel to experience what "normal" women went through—the eager anticipation of a positive pregnancy test, the ecstasy of getting one, and responding with something other than, "Nooooooooooooooooooooo!"

When people threw out the common "Gonna try for a boy?", my dear husband would flip his baseball cap backward and grin, "We ain't tried *yet*." Then he'd nudge me and crack a joke about "Fertile Myrtle."

While I was waiting to feel the urge to try for number three, Dave got it. He began hinting about how nice it would be to have another little Bogdan running around. I had been asking (OK, nagging) Dave to finish converting our basement into a family room. So we struck a deal: I'd help him work on a baby when he started working on the basement.

He got to work that week. And I aced another home pregnancy test that same week.

Nine months later I pushed twice and had a third girl—Rebecca Faith. I was so excited over another "drive-through" labor and delivery that I grabbed the cell phone to call my parents before taking a look at the child.

Child bearing had become a relaxing, two-day getaway in a place where I didn't have to cook or clean. My world didn't turn upside down as it had with the first two babies. I was "ready" this time. With two kids under my belt I felt like Pro Mom. I had no time for postpartum blues. And I had all the help I needed (and more) from four- and five-year-olds Sarah and Anna.

Baby Rebecca was low maintenance, bouncing up and down in her Johnny Jump Up all day, her fat, rosy cheeks jiggling to the beat of her pudgy feet tapping the floor. Three was so much easier than two had been. I had two "little mommies" to back me up whenever I couldn't get to Rebecca right away.

Time flew by. Soon I would once again have all kids—no babies!

"Three's My Limit!"

I became known for the easy childbirths the womenfolk in my family had experienced for generations. People frequently asked me how many more children I planned on having, as if my athletic abilities in the delivery room gave me reason for having a tribe of kids.

"Might as well keep going," they'd grin. I was mercifully able to refrain from committing aggravated assault in those moments.

I always declared, "Three's my limit!" I had friends who homeschooled five or six kids, baked homemade bread, raised goats, sewed quilts, and sang hymns by the fireplace at night. Obviously they had the "four-or-more call." But God had other things in mind for me. Too many children, I felt convinced, would prevent His "higher" plans for my life from coming to fruition. My goal was to get my babies raised and out of the house, so I could get back to my life.

During that time I wrote in my journal:

I dream of spending endless hours relaxing at a computer, typing away at a future best seller. I long to sit down and work on my book. That's what I want to do when I grow up. Oh? I'm already grown up? And I'm not an author who travels, speaking about what she's written? I'm a mother instead? You mean I spend my days picking up things that will end up back on the floor the next day and the next? No! I don't want that for a career. I want to write books and speak. I want to travel the country giving inspirational talks to mothers who spend *their* days picking up things that end up back on the floor the next day and the next. I want the satisfaction of knowing I'm encouraging, relating to, and empathizing with my audiences. I love the thrill of looking at their faces and seeing understanding tears as they listen to my stories. That's what I wish I were doing. Not this.

Little did I know, having more children than planned was one of God's keys to my spiritual maturation and preparation for a future call to ministry.

Tie Me Up!

Dave seemed to warm up quickly to the idea of having a large family. "What's a few more?" he often said. (Parenting is so easy when you're not home with the kids most of the day.)

I glared at him and yelled over the screams of fighting siblings, "Yeah, great idea; let's have a few more!"

During quieter moments, when the subject came up, I built my case masterfully, convincing Dave I couldn't handle any more kids. I was fit to be tied, and so were my fallopian tubes. His choice was clear: "tie me up" now or "lock me up" later, in a psyche ward. He agreed the former option made more sense, and we scheduled a consultation with an OB/GYN.

Sitting on an examination table four floors below the room where my babies were born, I asked the doctor about reversals. "If you're even thinking about that," he warned, "you shouldn't go through with this." I suspected he was right, but I told him I wanted to proceed anyway.

I walked down the hall for pre-op blood work. Before the nurse left the room to send my blood sample to the lab, she told me a technician would call by the end of the day if the results revealed I happened to be pregnant.

I knew I was supposed to hope for a negative blood sample. But as I folded clean towels back at home, I listened intently for the phone, wishing—strangely enough—that it would ring.

It didn't. My surgery was scheduled for the following week.

For the next few days my mind whirled with worry over whether I'd someday regret my decision. I couldn't imagine I ever would, but I'd heard stories about women waking up one day heartbroken over their loss of fertility. Could that happen to me, the woman who said, "No!", every time the pregnancy test came out positive? For about five minutes I'd consider canceling the appointment, then for the next five minutes I'd be dead set on tubal ligation. Then I'd doubt again.

I asked a friend, "How many kids do you think we should have?"

"Four," she replied matter-of-factly. That's how many she had.

I didn't know whether to love or hate her answer. No one should tell you how many children to have. You can ask, but they should never tell.

My surgery was scheduled for 7:00 a.m. on Friday, May 31, 2002. That morning, instead of getting dressed, I called the hospital. "I can't do this," I told the receptionist. "I'm not coming in."

She agreed it was better for me to realize this right now than a few hours—or years—too late. I hung up the phone, finally at peace. "This doesn't mean I have to have another baby," I reminded myself. I rubbed my hands together in satisfaction and made some toast.

Answering "the Call"

The following Labor Day I missed my period. I took another pregnancy test. (I'm going to petition Costco to sell them in bulk—especially since I once asked one of my small girls if she knew what one was, and she said she'd tried one out already—kids get curious about things stored in the bathroom cabinet. It came up negative.) When that menacing pink line appeared once again, I prayed, "Lord, I've asked You to make me that woman with a 'meek and quiet spirit' (1 Pet. 3:4). If this is what it takes to change me—having all these kids—You're letting me take the easy route. You could allow some other form of suffering to soften me—illness, economic hardship, tragedy—but You're leading me gently, and for that I thank You. I will gladly walk this road." I blubbered the words aloud and swallowed my newest reality like one might choke down a spoonful of cod liver oil.

Dave walked in from work that evening and asked, "What's the verdict?"

"We're going to have another baby." I forced a smile.

He laughed with pleasure and hugged me. He had reacted that way every time. As I stood there in his embrace, I couldn't help calling to mind a greeting card I'd once been given: on the front was a Photoshopped picture of a man sporting a woman's pregnant belly. The inside read, "Let him have the next one."

I gave birth to Ruth Esther the following April, surrounded by girlfriends cheering me through each push: "Go Faith! Go Faith!" We brought her home to join three sisters, and my "life verse" became Psalm 3:1: "Lord, how they have increased who trouble me!" (NKJV).

"Queendom" of Four

It's true what they say: "Never say 'never.'" I once said I'd never have kids. Then I said, "Well, not girls." And then, "OK, girls, but no more than three." Then, "Fine! I'm the mother of four children, but I will *never* be one of those homeschooling mothers who gathers eggs from the barn and makes scrapbooks on the side!"

The next thing I knew, I was homeschooling two daughters while chasing a toddlerette and balancing a baby girl on my hip. We owned twenty-four hens, and I became addicted to scrapbooking. I'm never going to say "never" again!

I traded in my slick red Chevy Cavalier for a Suburban laden with hardened raisins and cold french fries. My once meticulously vacuumed carpet was strewn with toys and dirty clothes. I couldn't get the theme song to *Veggie Tales* out of my head, and I considered sitting on the front porch alone with Dave for five minutes a *hot date.*

But I'm not complaining. Anna, Sarah, Rebecca, and Ruthie are the four best detours our lives ever took. Before I talk about God's role in unexpected detours (see chapter 3), let me introduce my lovely young ladies to you.

Anna is the gentlest thing to come along since her daddy. And she's just like him—practical, compliant, and emotionally even-keeled. When I had her, it was as if I gave birth to my left brain, providing for a peaceful and complementary relationship with my now fifteen-year-old daughter. I enjoy our discussions about possible career paths she may choose in science, even though I have to pretend that I know what I'm talking about. Anna is a no-drama girl who would rather be reading up on wilderness survival, for example, than gabbing on the phone. She's a sensible teenager who looks forward to getting her driver's license so that she will finally feel safe in the same car as her mother. Mature beyond her years, Anna is becoming as much a friend as a daughter.

Fourteen-year-old Sarah is just like—you guessed it—her mother. She's sensitive, spirited, and full of things to say to the world. She'd much rather write a riveting tale in her journal than do math, especially if she can nibble on cookies while doing so. A keen observer of human nature, Sarah is willing to step inside a person's head and see the world through that individual's eyes. Her tender heart and creative fingers are often at work making someone a homemade card or gift, sewing doll clothes for her sisters, or teaching little cousins how to string up a homemade fishing pole. She's a deep thinker with a passionate interest in books and the world of ideas, and a lookout tower for the underdog. Sarah's love for words and the pen makes her my writing buddy—and my clone (more about that later).

Rebecca is another Anna. She's my "big ole ten-year-old" who goes with the flow and keeps the world together (the world being Ruthie, according to Ruthie). "Let it go, Ruthie," she'll quietly command, and everything will instantly calm down. Rebecca has a dry, sarcastic sense of humor and doesn't waste words. Despite being the third child, she has the drive and focus of a firstborn executive. She takes pride in finishing chores and homework in record time. We call her "the Finder" and "the Reminder." If something has gone missing, Rebecca will find it. If I need to be reminded of something later, Rebecca, who is of sound mind more often than the rest of us, commits it to memory. She's your classic "calm, cool, and collected" kid, and I'm not sure which one of those she's more of.

To continue the pattern, Ruthie is like "Sarah"—the queen of story, inhaling the first word of every sentence in skin-blushed earnest. She is a continual stream of affection in the form of tight squeezes, kisses, and "I love yous" purred several times an hour. If Sarah has important things to say to the world, Ruthie has already said them a dozen times over. I can't wait to see what becomes of her someday, if I survive *her* to see it. Until then, I'm enjoying the ride, bumpy though it may be at times, parenting a now nine-year-old who is going on twenty-two. And what a wild, fun ride it is! Ruthie is the "family pet," the "class clown," and resident drama diva all in one. There's a wrinkle or laugh line on my face for every minute spent with Ruthie, and it's worth it.

There's no doubt in my mind that God intends for me to grow my four princesses into queens of grace and inner beauty. Isn't that the hope and purpose of a mother—to produce offspring beneficial to society?

Knowing this, I've struggled to understand why God appointed *me* to govern this "queendom" of four. Wouldn't a woman who had always dreamed of becoming a mother be better suited for the job?

It seems unfair—a cruel reality of life—that women who desperately want children often can't conceive, don't have the emotional support of family and friends, or have to stop having babies because of medical implications or nightmarish pregnancies, labors, and deliveries.

And there's me. My last three childbirths pretty much involved chatting a few minutes with the hospital staff before suddenly announcing, "It's time to push!" I'd hop onto the delivery bed, spit out my gum, and have a baby. Then we'd order pizza.

Life isn't always explainable, but God obviously had a special reason for making sure I had lots of kids. It wasn't because I could push them out faster than the doctor could change his clothes. God knew I needed a heart softening, and having four children would be the perfect tenderizer.

I am living proof that even the most self-centered woman can make a 180-degree turn and love having kids. It didn't happen overnight. At times it has been two steps forward and one step back. One of my girls once introduced me to a woman by saying, "This is my mom, and she doesn't like children." She muffled a giggle as she said it. Still, I realized I had a long way to go toward becoming a mother whose very disposition, at any time of day or night, or in any year of my life, reflects Jesus's words: "Suffer with little children—" I mean, "Suffer the little children...to come unto me" (Matt. 19:14, ASV).

 Refrigerator Magnet: God thinks I am going to be a great mom.

 Heart Exam: What part of being a mother do I find disappointing?

Chapter 3

THE GOD WHO EXPECTS THE UNEXPECTED

THIS CHAPTER IS dedicated to all of my friends who understand firsthand that a positive pregnancy test is not always welcome news. If you don't fit that category, I hope you read it anyway. Someone you know, or will know, does. Arm yourself with insight and wisdom to know how to help. Besides, this chapter answers the tough questions we all ask in life—questions about God's role in suffering, our free will, and His sovereignty. It is my prayer that no matter who you are, you will come away from this chapter with a deeper understanding of the ways of God.

♡ ♡ ♡

My friend Kitty took her twelve-year-old daughter, Katrina, on a weekend cabin getaway to have "the talk." After the two of them listened to a CD on the birds and the bees, Kitty explained to her daughter, in detail, how Katrina and her three siblings were conceived.

Katrina's jaw hit the floor at the revelation. "You mean you and Dad had to do that *four times?*" If only family planning were that simple.

Unspoken Questions

When I announced to friends and family, barely past postpartum blues, that baby number four was on the way, I heard everything from "Praise the Lord!" to "I'm so sorry." I imagined the unspoken questions and comments about my brood:

- "Doesn't she know how to use birth control?"
- "I wonder if this one was planned."
- "Did she mean to do this?"
- "Poor thing!"
- "I wonder if she's learned her lesson."
- "Better her than me!"

I rarely indulge people in tidbits about our family planning. I usually explain matter-of-factly that I had two sets of playmates with a nice four-year break in between. Admiring mothers often reply, "My, you planned that well!" Of course, not a single one of my pregnancies was well thought out—not by Dave and me, anyway.

Perhaps you've wondered if God was surprised by your little junior. I've struggled with that question many times—during my own pregnancies and while observing mothers whose quivers are much fuller than mine.

I sat in a church nursery one day with a woman and four of her grandchildren—ages four, three, two, and four months. Given the kids' age spans, I surmised that at least one of these children, like mine, may have been conceived unexpectedly.

The infant had a twin in long-term intensive care, and the mother was struggling to find child care so she could spend time with the hospitalized baby. My heart ached as I listened to the dear grandmother's story. I felt compassion, but at the same time I wondered, "Is her poor daughter going to keep having babies?"

Another time I ran into an old acquaintance at the grocery store. She had acquired three more kids since I'd seen her last (when she had five). All eight looked like they needed a bath and a good hair brushing. She looked ready to ram the shopping cart into the bread rack.

When I have these encounters, I'm almost tempted to wonder, "Should she have had that many kids?" I wonder if they ever ask themselves the same question.

I want to hold these stressed-out moms in my arms and tell them everything will be OK and that each one of their children is a precious gift from God. But is that always the case?

Tough Questions

The question may be easy to answer for those moms who lead their rows of prim ducklings through every phase of life with ease. I imagine there is never the slightest doubt that those sugar dumplings are "GOD's best gift" (Ps. 127:3, THE MESSAGE). When those kids sit in church or in the dentist's lobby—hands folded, back straight—their moms never have to ask themselves questions about God and conception. They cheerfully answer the "four or more" call.

But my rapidly multiplying ducklings were far from being "all in a row." I spent Sunday mornings in a church nursing room while Dave handled restless toddlers in the hall. I wondered why we bothered going to church when the piled-high laundry at home called louder than the preacher's voice over the crackling loud speaker.

And there's the disabled mom who's expecting again, or the frazzled mother of multiples who wonders if there's any chance her husband will ever take the night shift for feeding. How about the mom who's tired of the stares and dumb questions concerning her special-needs child?

What about you? On those really bad days do you cry because it's hard to be a nice mom, especially if you weren't thrilled about the idea of being a mom in the first place? I've seen tears of uncertainty well up in mothers' eyes as they wonder aloud if their children really were from God.

Or maybe you were thrown off the love-all-your-kids course by that one positive pregnancy test that occurred at the most inconvenient time in your life. I heard one mother declare within earshot of her fourth (and unplanned) child, "He came along and messed it all up!" The poor boy was already in elementary school, and I shuddered to think of the ill effects that such mutterings might have on his self-image. But I also empathized with the mom. The sad reality is that an unexpected pregnancy can sometimes lead to a less-loved child.

When the going gets tough, the tough questions get going:

- "Why me?"

- "Why now?"

- "What could I be doing with my life if I weren't so tied down?"

- "Why weren't we more careful?"

- "Did God do this or did we?"

I had always believed that every child conceived was planned by God—that is, until I started meeting mothers who acted more like bunnies than "responsible" human beings. Then I turned into a bunny. Before I knew it, I became a nose- and bottom-wiping, robed-and-slippered zombie. It wasn't the job I'd put in for.

Designer Baby

One day I poured out my sob story to a wise friend. She listened compassionately to my grievances over the loss of sleep, sanity, talent, romance, and routine. I blubbered to her that life was passing me by, taking all my dreams and potential with it as I watched beneath the load of babies that held me back. By that point in my life I was sure I was supposed to be preaching, not changing diapers. I asked her, "How can I be certain this is what God planned for me?"

"Write down your sermons and save them," she said. "God is too wise to be mistaken. He wasn't surprised by those positive pregnancy tests. He fashioned each union of sperm and egg into a design in accordance with His perfect will and infinite wisdom. If it was an 'oops,' it was *God's* well-planned 'oops.'"

That was it! Hadn't I grown up reciting verses like Psalm 139:13–16: "You made all the delicate, inner parts of my body, and knit them together in my mother's womb....You were there while I was being formed in utter seclusion! You saw me before I was born and scheduled each day of my life before I began to breathe" (TLB).

And there was Jeremiah 1:5, where God told the prophet, "I knew you before you were formed within your mother's womb; before you were born I...appointed you as my spokesman to the world" (TLB).

Did I not learn in Sunday school that God is the Master Designer of every minute detail of every person—from freckle count to disposition to number of days? He knew each of us personally and had a plan for our lives before we were conceived.

Of course, that is easy to believe when you have a perfect baby. Or if your finances are in place to raise a family. If the father is around. If you're mature enough. Healthy enough. Young enough.

If you've got it all together, even your unplanned pregnancy must have been God's "perfect will"—right? A designer baby sent by God. But what about other moms in different circumstances?

Octomom

Enter the "Octomom." You may remember Californian Nadya Suleman, the mother of six who conceived a set of octuplets in 2009 through in vitro fertilization while unemployed and receiving public assistance. Many people—from the common taxpayer to Dr. Phil— expressed outrage at Nadia and her fertility doctor.

A protest was held outside her home, a baby car seat thrown through her van window, and her public relations group received death threats. Meanwhile a kindhearted friend of mine knitted blankets for each of Nadya's babies and shipped them off to California.

As I watched the varied reactions to Nadya's story, I wondered where God fit into the picture. Was God directly involved in the conception of these eight test-tube babies? Or are Jonah, Jeremiah, Josiah, Makai, Isaiah, Noah, Nariyah, and Maliyah a series of eight mistakes— embryos thawed and developed at the hands of a greedy doctor and a foolish mother? How does God view the octuplets?

Perhaps there is a third option. Perhaps God did not direct Nadya Suleman to a fertility clinic any more than He directs pregnant women to take harmful birth-defect-causing drugs. Yet He stepped into that moment in which eight human beings were conceived: eight personalities— people with feelings, abilities, and futures. And because He is a God who knows the end from the beginning, and He is big beyond our understanding, He turned man's conception into God's remarkable creation.

Theologians will debate God's sovereignty versus man's free will until the end of the age because we are too small-minded to see the balance. We are bound by time; hence, a person's life has "a beginning"—at conception. But God exists outside of time and has no beginning and no end, and He sees each one of us as eternal beings. As with Jeremiah, He had a purpose for each of us before we came into the world, or the womb.

Though Nadya Suleman took it upon herself to be a single mom to fourteen children (free will), God knew each of those kids before they were conceived (sovereignty).

He didn't freak out over Suleman's choices. If one of her children someday finds a cure for cancer, God will have the last laugh.

Tragedy—Where Does God Fit In?

In the Bible we read that "God does not show favoritism" (Acts 10:34) and "sends rain on the righteous and the unrighteous" (Matt. 5:45). Far be it from me to try to completely comprehend God's will concerning your baby and mine. Whether it was an accidental pregnancy or a child born with special needs—I believe that until we understand how God views "surprise babies," we may not be able to love our children to the extent intended by the Creator.

Yes, the Creator. God is present at and aware of every conception. If a sparrow doesn't fall to the ground without His notice (Matt. 10:29), certainly God's Spirit hovers over each one of us while we are being "formed in utter seclusion...woven together in the dark of the womb" (Ps. 139:15, NLT). This includes every deformed child and every healthy child. Every drug-induced conception. Every baby conceived out of wedlock. Every single, double, or triple "oops." Every last-minute family surprise.

Am I suggesting that God directly orchestrates certain events—the child with spina bifida or Down syndrome, or the stillborn? And how about that perfectly-healthy-but-oh-so-unplanned and ill-timed baby?

No. God doesn't wake up each morning and say, "Whose life can I make miserable today?" That's what Satan does. Birth defects, miscarriages, and promiscuous teenage pregnancies are a part of this fallen world. As the Creator, God put in women the ability to get pregnant given the right conditions, and He is ever present through the whole process, as the Scriptures tell us. *But under His watchful eye, things still happen.*

Just ask the man Job. And the sparrows. Or that guy in the Gospel of John who was born blind. Jesus's disciples asked the Lord, "Who sinned, this man or his parents, that he was born blind?" (John 9:2).

Whose fault was it that your baby was born that way? Not enough folic acid? Was it your age? Who's to blame for this pregnancy? You shouldn't have left that diaphragm in the drawer. You should have known better than to walk across the campus alone at night.

Small-minded, we are just like Jesus's disciples, viewing life through our tiny lenses and trying to understand everything with our pitiful human reasoning. We are quick to cast blame—on ourselves, on others, and on God.

Jesus answered His disciples, "Neither this man nor his parents sinned...but this happened so that the work of God might be displayed in his life" (John 9:3).

Here is the hope and the place where two sides of truth meet: God uses plans gone awry as *the raw materials for His good purposes.* He is just and redeeming in nature. In the end everyone who belongs to Him (through belief in Jesus as Savior)—no matter the circumstances of one's natural birth—will be made whole and given perfect bodies to enjoy forever. (Satan will rot in hell, permanently disabled and, I imagine, eternally suffering with morning sickness and back labor.)

Remember, God is big and we are small—small in our perspectives and understanding. His will—His desire—is to receive glory (honor, fame) through *every human life.* That glory may come through a miraculous healing or through the miracle of a person glorifying God in the midst of suffering or in the humble sacrifice of the parents He appointed to raise that child.

God has never been and will never be baffled by what takes place in the womb. He is no more surprised by the life He creates than a potter is surprised by the rugged clay he uses to carefully mold a fine vessel with his skillful hands. God is never caught unawares when a child of His thoughts suddenly enters the realm of life—no matter how that child occurred or appears.

So, in a sense, that surprise baby you thought the stork dropped in was actually custom made from earthen material, raw humanity—a treasure in a fragile vase of clay. (See 2 Corinthians 4:7.) It was marked "special delivery" and shipped out by God Himself. *But it's in the sense that God allowed that child to be born to you because He has purposes in mind beyond your understanding.*

No matter what, God loves you and He loves your baby, far more than you can fathom. He is good. His heart and His character are good. He can be trusted. (More on that soon.)

A Win-Win Situation

Surprise sucklings can be hard to welcome when you returned from your honeymoon only nine months ago. Or if your local newspaper just hailed you as the oldest expectant woman in the county. Or if, like me, you just don't like surprises. And when they're delivered hungry and crying into your comfy (or chaotic) lifestyle, you can't help but feel a sense of "letdown."

Many who have experienced unwanted pregnancies or had unplanned children are tempted to see their kids as interrupters. They not only interrupt sleep, sex, phone conversations, and showers, but they can also single-handedly ruin career plans, hobbies, and education goals. Who wouldn't resent that?

Who ever said to herself, "Thank my lucky stars! I'm having a baby just when I'm about to graduate from medical school. Maybe the nurses can watch him while I operate." Or, "Welcome to our cozy single-wide, sweetie! Kiss your four siblings nighty-night, and I'll see if I can park you in the shower stall." When unwelcome surprises come our way, we're prone to ask, "How does *this* fit into my plans?"

I believe God has an answer for these misgivings. It may take a while to fully grasp. That's OK. God is patient, and He understands we don't always "get" things right away. But Romans 8:28 gives us the prescription for those "post-oops blues," and it yields no side effects. The wording of *The Message* paraphrase is particularly intriguing: "He knows us far better than we know ourselves, knows our pregnant condition.... That's why we can be so sure that every detail in our lives of love for God is worked into something good."

Every detail. For good! For the good of yourself, your children, and those whose lives you'll impact when you grab hold of this promise. God has a specific purpose for you and your baby. You may not understand what He's doing right now. But sooner or later you'll see it. God will follow through on His promise to work this out for good.

His only requirement from you is a simple, childlike trust. Rest in the assurance that your Father in heaven knows what He's doing and has your best interest at heart. That kind of faith is what releases God to work even the most hopeless situations out for good.

Your surprise pregnancy may have turned your world completely upside down. You may wish you could turn back the clock and return to your original plans. Forget it. You have now entered a win-win situation in which God not only saw the unexpected about to happen but also allowed it to fall right into place with His purposes for your life.

So tell your other gifts and callings to hang tight. You have a new and more important project to tend to for a while. And you may just discover it's the highest calling of all.

A Change of Plans

I never wanted to be a mom. I didn't play with dolls. I never babysat. Babies screamed when I held them in my awkward teenage arms. It was obvious to me that motherhood wasn't my destiny.

I married a minister and settled comfortably in a church pew, uninterrupted by kids. I loved my freedom. But one day I heard an inner voice loud and clear say: *"I want you to be a mom."* I tried to close my ears, but the words hounded me night and day. I heard them in radio broadcasts, magazine articles, sermons. I cried through Sunday services. The voice was so relentless I considered leaving the church, except pastor's wives don't do that sort of thing.

I shared my struggle with a few close friends. They advised me to "say yes to God" about motherhood. "If you haven't gotten pregnant by now, it'll surely take at least a year," they said. That would give me time to work things out in my heart. My husband happily agreed to the plan—another sign that God was speaking.

It took less than a year—one night, to be exact. I cried some more. I told God that if I had to be pregnant, I didn't want to be pregnant alone. He answered swiftly again; that fall six mothers in our church had babies within a few weeks.

I'll never forget kneeling at the altar, hearing an almost audible voice say, "I want you to be a godly mom."

"But I don't know how!" I blurted out.

"The Holy Spirit will show you how," God promised.

Six kids and seventeen years later, I was shocked when a friend said to me one day, "You are such a godly mom." I could hardly contain my emotions as I thought back to that day at the altar. God had kept His promise!

—VERNA LAIN

Redemption

An unexpected pregnancy may be all fine and good if you're happily married and can "afford" children. Sure, a sudden "family surprise" can throw you for a loop. But once you get past the landmarks of sleeping through the night and potty training, you can make it with an extra kid.

For some women, though, an unexpected pregnancy is devastating for unique reasons. Perhaps you're the young mother of a child born out of wedlock; maybe you're the pastor's daughter and were involved in what turned out to be a one-night stand. While everyone at church is still reeling from the shock of your pregnancy, you're on a get-away bus reeling with morning sickness.

Maybe a rape from a decade ago is robbing you and your husband of the love life you think you'll never have. The child of that assault is a permanent reminder of the crime that was committed against you.

Whatever your situation, whether you were "at fault" in the conception or not, guilt can blind you to the right perspective. Guilt can cause any mother to see her life as one big disaster. I'm not going to tell you to just get over it and move on with your life. But I do want you to know that God sees the bigger picture, and He wants you to see it too.

Genesis 38 tells of a woman named Tamar. What a soap opera life she had! Her husband died. Her father-in-law gave her his other son in order to "raise up seed" to her dead husband, as was the custom, but he failed to fulfill his obligation. Then her second husband died too. Desperate for offspring to carry on the family name, Tamar posed as a prostitute and waited for her father-in-law to walk by. Deception led to conception. She bore his illegitimate son and named him Perez.

But Perez ended up in the genealogy of Jesus! (See Matthew 1:3.) Would God allow His Son to have such corruption in His ancestry? Yes, indeed.

While we're examining the Messiah's lineage, let's check further down in Matthew's list. There's Boaz, whose mother, Rahab, is believed to have been a prostitute (v. 5). And there's Solomon, whose parents had engaged in an adulterous affair (v. 6).

I believe God let us in on the facts surrounding these

conceptions in order to show us the meaning of *redemption*. Can God truly turn our worst blunders or life's greatest sin-tragedies into something good? I believe so. In fact, I stake my faith on it.

Redemption is central to God's nature. To me the word means I don't live life ruled by the guilt from my failures. I let God make something beautiful of them. Nor do I wallow in the slough of *would'ves, could'ves,* and *should'ves.* When I understand redemption, there's no need to go on wondering what could have been. I can look with hope at what God is doing now. I can wait with expectation for the bright tomorrow He'll shape out of a miserable past. I believe this is possible for any mom in any circumstance.

But we have to believe that we have been redeemed and then live out that belief through—as the passage quoted previously in Romans 8 states—a life lived with "love for God."

Long before we were born, God looked into our futures and saw each dreadful mistake we'd ever make. Knowing we'd be taken captive by ensuing guilt and despair, He ransomed us with the blood of His Son. Any shame or disillusionment we suffer is evidence of a failure to understand and accept that plan.

God bought us back from and made up for our mishaps. And when He makes up for things, He does a thorough job. God loves to take the grossness of our mistakes and turn it into something that will "wow" the world. God-lovers call this "grace."

At times I have struggled to comprehend this. I've pondered teenagers making "pregnancy pacts," for example, and asked myself, "How can I reconcile those girls' foolish choices with God's preordained plan for their precious babies?"

But that's what redemption is all about. It's about God foreseeing the Eves who will take the bite of forbidden fruit and appointing a Savior to pay on the cross the price of pardon. But it doesn't stop there. Everything taken for ruin can be converted into something of beauty and value. "Bouquets of roses instead of ashes" (Isa. 61:3, THE MESSAGE)—that's redemption. You can't go wrong, even when you've gone wrong.

Perhaps you can't imagine that God could make something good from your unplanned pregnancy. I can't imagine attempting motherhood without Him. I would have needed God's help even if I *was* that doting mother who always dreamed of having a large family. How much more do I need someone who can help me find pleasure in what I never purposed and strength for the task?

If this is all new to you, you may want to start from square one. Invite God into your life and ask Him to begin the redeeming process. (I'll talk more about this in chapter 14.) Watch Him start weaving every detail of your circumstances into a beautiful tapestry that testifies to His power, as you remain surrendered to Him. Let Him bury your blunders in the sea of redemption. Your kids will thank you for it. So will their kids. The blessings of faith will continue through generations if God's transforming power is switched on and allowed to affect change in who you are as a mom.

Refrigerator Magnet: God wants to make my life a win-win situation.

 Heart Exam: Do I fully understand and accept God's desire to redeem my life? If not, whom can I talk with about it?

Chapter 4

THAT'S WHAT LITTLE MOMS ARE MADE OF

BACK IN THE time of BC, I was CCC (before children, I was calm, cool, and collected). Dave is a relatively quiet man, a good listener, and extremely patient. For whatever reason, that makes him and me fairly complementary and compatible. So when we were childless, I could have almost passed for one of those sweet and quiet women (except during the occasional hormonal uprising). At least I wanted to think I was pleasant to be around. I loved myself! I didn't know myself.

The Israelites of old didn't know what they were made of either before God allowed them to be pushed to their limits in the Sinai desert. It had been easy to be nice little Hebrew children when life was going their way. But they got a rude awakening when God took them through forty long years of blistering wilderness heat with only manna for breakfast, lunch, and dinner.

That ordeal exposed them for who they really were, and it wasn't pretty: "In the desert the whole community grumbled against Moses and Aaron. The Israelites said to them, 'If only we had died by the LORD's hand in Egypt! There we sat around pots of meat and ate all the food we wanted, but you have brought us out into this desert to starve this entire assembly to death'" (Exod. 16:2–3).

Of course, they weren't really starving. God had literally blown in a hailstorm of birds and continued the blizzard of bread-flakes—cereal from the sky every morning. The only problem was that it wasn't exactly what the people ordered. I can relate. I entered my own wilderness in 1997, the year I became a mother. And it wasn't quail that put me in a "fowl" mood. Staying home all day every day with four energetic teeny-weeny-boppers was the telltale mirror that exposed me for who I really was.

Life has a way of doing that. For example, my friend Verna once volunteered to take Anna and Sarah for a while so I could catch up on the housework. I was nice to everyone in the house all morning. That's because half of them were gone and the other half were napping. But when the bickering duo came traipsing in with muddy boots and woke up the babies, my disposition changed. The woman who hummed sweetly as she waltzed with the mop only minutes ago was suddenly on a red-faced, vein-popping rampage, slashing everyone in her path with loud and venomous words.

I'm convinced all children are on a mission from God to expose the monsters lurking behind mothers' pretty masks. The moment we think we've finally obtained that "meek and quiet spirit" (1 Pet. 3:4, KJV), an act of violence erupts between two siblings, causing the soggy contents of a cereal bowl to cascade over the dining table and onto someone's book. Suddenly the roaring lion within—the one we thought we'd caged for good—is unleashed, doing its damage to our children and shocking, disappointing, and discouraging us.

Why does God constantly make us face the painful reality that we don't have it all together? Because otherwise we wouldn't realize how much we need Him.

Cruisin' for a Bruisin'— the Value of a Felt Need

I experienced a whole week of this lack of "felt need" when Dave and I went on a Caribbean cruise one summer. We left one- and two-year-olds Ruthie and Rebecca with a sitter and took six- and seven-year-olds Sarah and Anna with us for a week of luxury aboard the largest cruise liner Royal Caribbean sails. And luxury it was. While passengers basked in the pleasantry of fine dining, hot tubs, and sandy beaches, I was tickled just to not change a diaper for seven days or be awakened before 7:00 a.m. And how I enjoyed my older girls without interruption by toddler antics! It felt like we were the all-American, easy-does-it family of four. Life was good—too good.

I faithfully read the Gideon Bible found in our cabin for the first few days. But other than that brief token of worship, I was managing just fine on my own. There were no housecleaning battles, no dinners to burn, no tight schedules to keep, no fights to referee, and no training pants to swish out in the toilet. I slept in every morning, soaked in the sun, and ate gourmet meals prepared by someone else.

Everything was going so well, I stopped bothering to take the Bible out of the nightstand drawer. There was simply nothing to drive me to it. I was being a nice mommy all by myself. I was cruisin' all right—cruisin' for a bruisin'.

Every seven-day cruise comes to an end. In no time I found myself dumped back into real life, facing so-called "Mount Never Rest," a formation of post-vacation laundry. Everyday stress and mess came back into my picture-perfect world. This mom's vacation was over, and so was my vacation from God. I realized once again that I just can't be the person I want to be without Him. And in His mercy He had made me a mom to show me that!

My personal call to motherhood was God's way of showing me what I'm really made of. It's not sugar and spice. It's hardly everything nice. I'm more like snakes and snails and puppy dog tails when it comes to the way I react when I find a pile of Chia Pet clippings scattered all over my just-vacuumed carpet.

Mother "Fail"

One night I was tucking Ruthie in and as usual was in hurry-up-and-go-to-sleep-so-I-can-get-on-with-my-life mode. She wanted to ask yet one more question, and I reluctantly agreed to let her. What she asked hit me with the force of a cannon ball.

"Mom, when are you going to be nice again?" She asked it in the same manner in which she might have inquired when we were going to go to the grocery store again. She literally wanted to know at what hour I would be making the switch to "nice mom."

Ouch.

Reality encounters like these have prompted me to

write journal entries like this one, written before Ruthie was even born:

> I feel like a failure as a mother. I'm harsh, sharp, quick-tongued, snappy, unloving, very impatient, and downright mean. I moan and groan like the worst whiner I never allow my kids to be.

I came to a breaking point one day and called my dad (my own personal Dr. Phil) for over-the-phone family therapy. I blubbered to him that I was not fit to be a mother, and I had no self-control when it came to dealing with childish behavior. I was ready to throw in the towel and go hide in a childless place, gorging on bags of peanut M&Ms for the next eighteen years.

He said, "Faith, your problem is you think life is about what you can accomplish. That's not true. Life is about *relationships.*"

That was a new revelation to this goals-driven woman with a type-A personality. I knew he was right. I needed a drastic change in perspective.

I'm a "list" person; I like to formulate a mental list of the next day's activities before I go to bed each night, and I write that list down on paper before my feet hit the floor each morning. But now I realized my lists needed to change from "Get the floor mopped...Get the laundry done..." to "Paint Sarah's nails" and "Listen to Chopin with Anna."

I knew this would be a real challenge for me. My sanity is directly linked to the general state of order in my physical surroundings. And if a visitor shows up without warning before I've cleaned the house, I might open the door and greet her with all the confidence of a woman shopping in her bathrobe.

Inspired by my dad's insight, I framed and hung a sign where visitors would see it as they entered my front door:

A TIDY HOUSE IS A SIGN
OF CHILD NEGLECT

But that didn't stop me from penning journal rants like this one:

> I cried for a while last night—I mean, *sobbed*. It all got to me. The chaotic office with guinea pig droppings all over the floor, car parts left unsold, canned goods, the whole nine yards of mess. Then there's the freezer—it's a danger zone with two-pound rocks of freezer-burned veggies ready to land on toes and break them the second you open the door. And the laundry room—will I ever see the surface of my washer and dryer again? I need a maid. It would be heaven to sit at the table and explain fractions to Sarah while someone makes my house shiny. It's beyond our budget, but I just might hire a housecleaning lady anyway. Sanity is worth the money.

I never did hire a maid. And I still struggle to keep my house at a tolerable level of cleanliness. There are plenty of times I forget my dad's advice and fall back into "all about me" mode. But as I learn the hard way that it's not worth it, days like these are becoming fewer and farther between:

My freezer looks good. I won't be embarrassed now if Alison opens it when she comes over for lunch. And an added bonus to my day—I attacked my stovetop with Easy Off and scrubbed the burner plates. Now the smoke alarm won't go off every time I heat up a burner. Clean freezer, clean stovetop—oh, and I even managed to mop the kitchen floor today. It's been at least a month. And we homeschooled—got most of the subjects done.

But I was Witch Mom today. Witch Mom has a sparkling clean kitchen. But Witch Mom has hurting children who are probably having bad dreams about being yelled at.

I guess it really is true—you can't have it all. At least *I* can't have a spotless house, a loving disposition, and happy children all at once. If I had a maid I could. But I don't. So I must choose either a happy house or happy children.

Thankfully the choice between a radiant house or radiant offspring is being made less and less. With diligent training, the kids are becoming little housekeepers themselves. As I transitioned into that wonderful phase of this journey, experiences like this one helped to make the ride smooth:

February 14

I must capture this feeling before it gets away.

I have given an entire day to the girls as their Valentine's Day gift. A whole day to do with me as they wish. I ignored the surrounding filth as we made cards, baked heart-shaped cookies, played Checkers, read in bed, and watched *Alice in*

Wonderland. They soaked up every minute with me—Anna commenting more than once that this was "the best Valentine's Day ever."

I tickled Ruthie and Rebecca and reveled in their giggles. I took pictures of the cards the girls and I made together. Anna killed me in Checkers and loved every minute of it. Sarah went to sugar heaven frosting cutout cookies. The four of us snuggled under layers of blankets at naptime and read *King Snake.*

It is now 11:30 pm. Since the girls went to bed I have managed to dry one load of laundry, run the scraps to the chickens, and sweep a thousand tiny beads that spilled during the card-making party. The rest of the house is still steeped in dirty neglect. Baskets of laundry wait in every corner— some dirty, some clean—all sentinels of hope in my good intentions.

I could have transformed the office into something usable and finally cleaned up the guinea pig mess. I could have done a lot with this house today. I could have that exhilarating feeling I get when I've started and finished a project and made a room shine. I could rest in knowing I'll wake up to a home as pristine as a winter sunrise. But I won't. I'll wake up to the call of chores undone and projects screaming silently for attention. I still can't see the surfaces of my washing machine and dryer.

But my girls are happy. I was a good mom today. They told me so. We were together—doing things together. I have created something permanent. A clean house is never permanent. The memory of this Valentine's Day is.

I feel good. So good. This is better than the I-got-so-much-done-today feeling I enjoy when I have tackled a long-overdue chore. There is an acute look-what-I-built-in-a-day and a they-will-never-forget-this contentment settling deep into my soul, giving me peace with myself and with God. I got *a lot* done today.

You may be one of those laid-back personalities who don't panic when unexpected company finds your house looking more like Oscar the Grouch's top-pick resort. How I envy those moms! What it must be like to live in harmony with clutter. But I have found that even the most soft-spoken, sugary-voiced mothers can get pushed to the point of exasperation on a daily basis. Even if it's not vocalized at glass-cracking ranges, we sure know how to let our children know we don't appreciate their interrupting our daily "me agendas." And an emotion-damaged child can send us packing our bags for a long guilt trip.

At times like these I'm ready to fire myself as a mother before my kids do. My only hope for a while was to realize the next day couldn't possibly be worse. It tends to not be, and so I'd be a little sugar and spice for a change—until the next bad day. Then the grace to "be good" that I felt the previous day was once again replaced with guilt over my bad behavior.

I call this phenomenon the "guilt-grace" roller coaster. When we're behaving well as moms, God likes us, and when we blow it, He disapproves and turns a cold shoulder, right? Isn't it all about performance? Making and keeping God happy with my level of mothering success? That's what I thought.

No More "Perfect Mom"

At age three, during naptime one day, my son Elijah was bored and decided to shred the first few pages of a treasured train book. I didn't take it well. I yelled, and when he opened his arms for a mercy-hug, I—MaryBeth Lynn—pushed my beloved firstborn son onto the bed. Of course, regret soon followed, and I hugged him and told him how sorry I was. But years later, I found a torn page from that book, and memories of the hurt I saw in his big, brown eyes returned to haunt me.

For all the years I hoped, dreamed, and obsessed about becoming a wife and mother, how could I have turned out to be so horrible? Anger had not been part of my plan. I'd spent years preparing myself, reading countless parenting books until, at age thirty-five, I enthusiastically embarked upon my homemaking journey.

Ten years in, I could almost hang my head in shame, looking back on more guilt-filled moments than I care to count. I'm all but convinced an alien took up residence in my body on the maternity ward. The creature is petty, mean, and demanding; it's not at all a friendly traveling companion.

But it does not define who I am.

As one who knows the love of God personally, I've come to understand His grace and forgiveness. I have confidence that as I do my part to humble myself and sincerely ask forgiveness from Him and my children, God is doing His part to change me. And it's not "Perfect Mom" He's changing me into, but a woman who is more like Him. "Christlike Mom"—that's what I am becoming as I give the tattered pages of my life to Him. In those moments when I feel the deepest regret for how far I fall short, He lets me know I'm still loved just the way I am. He sees my flaws, and despite them He is making me into the mother my family needs.

—MARYBETH LYNN

"Walking in the Spirit" and How I Got It All Wrong

One weekend Dave and I left the girls with a sitter and attended a Joyce Meyer convention at the Giant Center in Hershey, Pennsylvania. I was impressed by the way she matter-of-factly spelled out how Christian salvation works in everyday life. She taught from Romans 8, where Paul tells us "there is now no condemnation for those who are in Christ Jesus...who do not walk according to the flesh but according to the Spirit" (vv. 1, 4, NAS).

I'd heard the passage all my life, even memorized it. But I hated the verse, really. To me it meant, "There is no condemnation to those who don't misbehave." That was no consolation to this short-tempered mom.

But Joyce shed new light on the subject. She explained that "walking in the Spirit" has little to do with one's behavior and everything to do with one's mind-set. I looked back at Romans 8:1 and put that verse in its proper context, connecting the last part of Romans 7 to the first part of chapter 8 for the first time in my life (I particularly like the way the International Standard Version puts it):

> For I have the desire to do what is right, but I cannot carry it out. For I don't do the good I want to do, but instead do the evil that I don't want to do. But if I do what I don't want to do, I am no longer the one who is doing it, but it is the sin that is living in me. So I find this to be a principle: when I want to do what is good, evil is right there with me. For I delight in the law of God in my inner being, but I see in my body a different principle waging war with the law in

my mind and making me a prisoner of the law of sin [which says I am condemned] that exists in my body. What a wretched [woman] I am! Who will rescue me...? Thank God through Jesus the Messiah, our Lord, because *with my mind I myself can serve the law of God, even while with my human nature I serve the law of sin. Therefore there is now no condemnation for those who are in union with the Messiah Jesus.*
—ROMANS 7:18–8:1, ISV, EMPHASIS ADDED

Or in the words of The Message Bible, there is no condemnation for those of us who, "instead of redoubling our own efforts, simply embrace what the Spirit is doing in us" (Rom. 8:4).

This was life changing for me. I understood the passage to mean that since I sincerely wanted to please God, as was evidenced by my having surrendered my life to Jesus and my commitment to seek Him daily, there was to be no more living under a dark cloud of guilt. God saw the *agony I was in over my sin.* I agonized to suffocating levels; guilt, like a snake, was squeezing the very life out of me while making absolutely no improvement in my behavior.

At one point, in her raspy voice, Joyce said, "Stop fellowshipping with sin!" She revealed that when we wallow in condemnation, it's like pulling up a chair next to Satan and sipping tea with him for the afternoon. A light came on. I had never truly "walked in the Spirit," and it had nothing to do with the fact that I was a mean mom! My thinking about my own power to be good was all wrong.

I want to be careful to make a distinction between

conviction and condemnation here: conviction is a good thing. It comes from the Holy Spirit and points out the areas of our life that need to change (my temper). Conviction should drive us to our knees to seek God's help. But it should *not* drive us to self-loathing; that's what condemnation does, because it comes from Satan. He wants us to join him in his hatred of us.

You know what? I refuse. Jesus's shed blood for me is too precious to waste. I will not "frustrate the grace of God" (Gal. 2:21, KJV) by not appropriating the finished work of the cross. My sin—*and the guilt it brings*—was nailed to that cross, and there it will stay. Guilt-ridden moms, we need to get over ourselves and start walking in the Spirit. We must embrace the work the Spirit is already doing in us.

Stepping Off the Roller Coaster

Joyce helped me discover the remedy for that guilt-grace roller coaster: it's getting out the tried-and-true Bible and not just reading it but pondering it throughout the day, meditating on what I've read. Meditation was very important to ancient Jews; it meant, literally, to ruminate like a cow. I was to take the scriptures that I knew so well and start chewing on them all day long—particularly the parts that speak about who God says I am.

God loves to tell me through the Scriptures what I'm like—the positives—much as I enjoy reiterating to each of my girls their respective strengths. I get tickled when I realize Sarah has inherited a writing ability, and I love telling her so, suggesting various careers in which she can use that talent someday. I know she soaks in the affirmation when I compliment the way she so skillfully weaves words together. And I'm fully aware that the more I tell her such things, the easier it will be for her to reach her God-given potential. She believes that what I say of her is true, and the more I say it, the more she becomes it.

It works the same way with my heavenly Dad and me. I can feel like "dragon lady" until I start to read what I'm like from His perspective. Mind you, He's a bit biased, me being His adopted daughter and all (Rom. 8:15), but basically I'm the apple of His eye (Deut. 32:10). He declares boldly (it's almost embarrassing) that I'm perfect (Heb. 10:14), able to do anything (Phil. 4:13), more precious than the world, and I have everything going for me. If I dare protest, He shushes me with His soothing voice (an inner "whisper") and tells me to rest in His unconditional love.

My prayer time is often spent imagining myself curled up and being rocked in God's lap, held close to His chest, clinging to folds of a linen robe as He caresses my hair. After a good while of soaking in this kind of assurance, I start acting like it's all true—what He thinks of me. Basic psychology teaches us that behavior springs from identity. In the natural I may bear the physical mark of a mad mother—a vertical frown line on my forehead—but in God's reality I'm a well-loved daughter of the King, and, little by little, I'm becoming the kind of person He says I already am.

I don't get discouraged when the monster within keeps rearing its ugly head. It's like the "Whack-a-Mole" game kids love to pound in video arcades. Every pesky little pop-up of a troublesome "mole" in my character is an opportunity to bash it with the mallet of God's Word. One of the blows I love to deliver is His promise to continue the work He's begun in me (Phil. 1:6), or the declaration that I am not condemned for my emotional outbursts as long as I am truly repentant and seeking to please God in my heart (Rom. 7:25; 8:1).

My faith muscles are strengthened through the pounding. I hold to the promise that eventually the enemy, my "old self," will be obliterated. The game will slow down and finally stop. I'll look at myself in amazement, realizing those ugly temper flare-ups have been eradicated. There are no more moles to whack.

Furthermore, those "moles" are more accurately explained as the "voice of accusation"—whether that inner voice comes from my own self or the devil. (Revelation 12:10 speaks of Satan as being our accuser.) We should pay no mind to those condemning words when we realize, as Paul explains in Romans 6:11, that our "old self," the person we are becoming less and less of as we trust in Christ, is reckoned—accounted for in the heavenly books—as *dead.* Why would one need to whack a dead mole? Hence, the whacking I speak of is not a religious exercise or laborious struggle as much as a declaration of faith and a resting in the truth that God is changing us for the better.

The "moles" that started creeping out of the inner recesses of my personality as soon as I heard my first newborn cry are many in number. But they all burrow down to the basic foundation called selfishness. My selfishness was manifested each time I stomped my weary feet down the hall to nurse a hungry baby at 3:00 a.m. Or when I shoved the baby back into the bassinet after a feeding so

I could tackle another chore, missing an opportunity to rock and hold her close. Or when I told my four-year-old that we'd read the story later. Most of my "just a minutes" were born of a selfish desire to push my agenda ahead of theirs.

From this root of selfishness stemmed anger, resentment, and self-pity. Anger because an unsettled child spoiled my plans to scrapbook after she was in bed. Resentment because a three-year-old early-riser robbed me of precious sleep. Self-pity because I had no quiet, uninterrupted time to write. Anger and resentment because my ambitions were constantly pushed onto the back burner.

I vividly remember the night Sarah called me upstairs for the twelfth time to ask for the twelfth drink and twelfth prayer. After practically slinging a cup of water in her face, I fumed as she asked me for another good night hug. My arm was suddenly a heavy, foreign object attached to my side. It was all I could do to make it wrap around her little body for a second. My hand refused to stroke her blonde curls, and a kiss would have definitely been asking for too much. I ended the forced hug and walked out realizing I was too selfish to love my daughter. Something had to change.

Ironically my children are the tools God is using to change me into being all they need. My kids need a loving, affirming, gentle, and patient mommy. I am hardly any of those things at times. I know this because they show me either by quiet retreat or acting out.

How do I change? In and through raising *them*, as I bring God into the process. How do I know I'm changing?

They continue to show me—by changing into happier kids as the result of me becoming a more godly mom. I had them for a reason.

 Refrigerator Magnet: Today I step off the guilt-grace roller coaster and rest in God's unconditional love for me.

 Heart Exam: Do I trust the power of God's love to change me?

Chapter 5

THE CHALLENGE CHILD

EVERY MOTHER SEEMS to have one kid who is especially challenging. I suspect that, as in my case, the "challenge child" for most moms is the one who takes after the mother. It's like raising a clone of yourself, a "mini me." I have one such child. I have "lost it" with her so often that only God will be able to take the credit for her becoming an emotionally whole, secure, and confident adult.

One Sunday I was sitting next to this particular daughter in church during Communion. Church can be a good place to lovingly connect with your kids and right any wrongs you may have committed toward them during the week. At church there are no piled-up wet washcloths left on the carpet by young hands and no forgotten smoothies waiting in the fridge to get tipped over and ooze brown scum through lettuce and eggs. There are no such potential hazards to parent-child relationships. So I thought I'd take advantage of the moment. I drew Challenge Child close as we held our Communion cups and fragments of matzo cracker.

I leaned in to her and attempted a unifying prayer: "Dear Lord, thank You so much for this opportunity to take Communion with my sweet daughter. Thank You for giving this precious girl to me. Thank You for Your blood that was spilled for our sins and that is now about to be spilled onto her lap if she does not stop wiggling. Please help her to sit still and drink her juice immediately before it stains her dress and ruins the carpet in Jesus's mighty name!"

"Creative Child"

A creative type, this daughter has better things to think about than combing out her tangled hair, for instance. Her mind travels to far more exciting places than the kitchen, where emptying the top rack of the dishwasher becomes a two-hour chore. She doesn't mean to be difficult or disobedient; she's not a strong-willed child. She's simply...dreaming.

I've dreamed at times too. I've had very bad dreams, of taking her by the ponytail and swinging her round and round, high in the air like a lasso, and then letting her go, sailing away, out of sight. In these horrible fantasies I never look to see where or how she will land. I don't wish the child harm. I love her to the moon and back, just as you do yours. I just want her away from me at times.

I know she picks up on this. One day we were riding in the car, and for some reason she was singing the phrase "There is no light!" over and over. It had to do with traffic lights, I believe. I quickly became annoyed and snapped her name.

"What?" She stopped singing. In a split second I recalled that mothers ought to be long-suffering, and I decided to turn my reprimand into something positive. So in the same high-pitched tone I said, "I love you!"

Confused, she asked, "What do you mean?" (Translation: "Don't you mean to scold me?") I realized I had another ten thousand miles and that many more years to go in becoming the mother I need to be.

I have needed to invent creative ways to make amends with this particular daughter of mine. Saying "I'm sorry, will you forgive me?" gets old after you repeat it several times a day. One time I held her close and whispered in her ear, "Is your forgiver working OK today?" Her lips curled slightly as she nestled in my arms.

I confess I've had to ask my daughter that question many times. So far her "forgiver" is still in good working order. Maybe it's because, by the grace of God, I've been somehow able to keep pointing her to the Great Forgiver.

Fly to Jesus!

I saw evidence of this leaning-into-Jesus on a particularly bad day calling for a therapeutic, long, windblown car ride in the country. I climbed into the Suburban, fuming, and put down the windows in hopes that the fresh air would blast away those fumes of anger, or at least drown the noise of backseat whiners adding to my angst. She'd been herself again: dreamy, weepy, disobedient, and basically impossible. I responded by being myself: out of control and bordering on emotionally abusive.

I floored the gas pedal and let the wind rip through us. "Impossible" sat next to me, her long, blonde hair blowing wildly about. I drove on and on to nowhere in particular, hoping the noise of nature would settle my emotions by the time we got there.

And then I heard another noise—a sweet, faint noise

carried along mighty gusts in the passenger window. It was my daughter's voice, singing a tone-deaf rendition of "Fly to Jesus." I slowed the car to get a better listen. "Fly to Je-sus, fly to Je-sus, fly to Je-e-sus and live!" she sang.

Something about the way *–sus* fell out of key gripped my heart. I strained to listen more, not turning toward her for fear she'd stop singing. On she went, happily crooning the same phrase—the only words to the song that she knew—over and over, as if she hadn't a care in the world. Tears spilled from my eyes.

Far from shrinking back from a potentially dangerous mother and shutting herself away from the world, my daughter had opened herself to the Source of comfort for all of us and led the way for me to be healed in His manifest presence. She'd flown right into the arms of the One who loved her unconditionally. Her song was evidence that she was still fully alive in His love, even when I'd failed her.

The Best Medicine

Life is a journey of daily choices, including how I choose to respond to my developmentally disabled son. At age thirty-two he is still living at home, and my days center around his supervision and care and the challenges he presents: his tendency to wander off and the rides home in the back of a police cruiser once he's been found; his unreasonableness at doctor, dentist, and haircut appointments; waiting with him, often three or more hours in restaurants, because he eats. so. slowly; hauling the water hose indoors with the nozzle set on power wash to clean Jon's shower because he squeezed long ribbons of shampoo all over it again; constant reminders for Jon to brush his teeth, put on clean clothes, and take his meds and the rock-solid resistance I encounter when he refuses.

Then there's the stuff that borders on ridiculous: like the day he attended his adult program with only the left side of his face shaved; his shopping for "a wife" in the Sears catalog; his taking karate lessons with vacuum cleaner hose "weapons" attached to his belt; his testing out the fire alarm during lunch hour in a crowded restaurant; and sporting crab-shaped kids' swim goggles on his head all day with no regard for his appearance. The list is endless.

Almost every hour, it seems, I am faced with a choice: Do I *react*—or do I *respond*? Do I give way to anger and subsequent self-pity, or do I allow peace and contentment to govern my words, thoughts, and actions toward this child God gave me?

A wise man once wrote, "A joyful heart is good medicine" (Prov. 17:22, ESV). As I watch Jon take his pills today, I smile and thank God for giving me the *best* medicine—His joy (Ps. 28:7).

—DIANE CONNIS

Raising My Clone

As I've already pointed out, Challenge Child is the daughter who is most like me. To illustrate: I was walking with her one day and noticed she looked at my feet and quickly shifted her step pattern to match mine—our left feet must hit the ground simultaneously. I well understood this requirement for a leisurely stroll; that is exactly the thing I sometimes do when Dave and I take walks together. Our steps must be in sync. Also, I notice she needs to push the "clear" button on the microwave if she walks by and happens to see the timer display is not reset; I can heat food only for a number of minutes that is a multiple of five.

One would think this knowledge would thwart any temptation on my part, during moments of exasperation, to book a one-way escape cruise to Fiji. But that is not the case.

I have a tendency to nitpick about everything the poor child does. As I was confessing this to a friend once, she said words I'll never forget and that may very well save my daughter's life: "Faith, just lay off of her."

Those words came to mind one evening as the six of us gathered in the family room to enjoy old homemade videos on VHS. There was one particular video in which she was about five, with those bouncing, white curls and an adorable inability to pronounce her "R's."

"Can I hold baby Woofie [Ruthie]?" she'd say. We were filled with "aww" as we watched our little Goldilocks on screen. She relished the attention, watching it with us at age twelve.

While filming a dinner scene in which everyone was talking loudly over one another, Dave had zoomed in on her with the camcorder. She was quietly, busily preparing an artful masterpiece—a three-story butter and pickle sandwich with toothpick scaffolding. Watching the video, I was just about to remark how cute her creation was when I heard myself—my old, recorded self—scold her.

"Stop that! You're wasting toothpicks." The dear girl quickly laid her sandwich building to rest and went back to eating dinner, trying hard to stay out of trouble.

My heart broke. I wanted to reach through the screen and hold her and show off that pickle sandwich to everyone. Instead, I watched myself continue policing table manners and toothpick usage. Shamed by my foolishness, I turned to a more grown-up daughter and begged forgiveness. There was evidence of hurt brimming in her eyes. I held her tightly, wishing back that long-ago evening.

"Do not be hard on your children, so that their spirit may not be broken" (Col. 3:21, BBE).

I'm the Same Way!

If Challenge Child were in a different family, she'd probably be on Ritalin for the way she can't seem to stay focused on a task. On plenty of days I've been tempted to get her the pills. But I consider the side effects and just can't. (I respect those who choose to go the medical route for the treatment of ADD.) So I take one day at a time and keep plodding through, sometimes hour by hour, trying to manage her behavior in addition to trying to manage mine.

One thing that helps me lighten up on her is realizing I have the *same issue*. Every time I see her take a glass from the dishwasher that she's supposed to have emptied in a matter of minutes and place it on the shelf, then turn to add another element to her drawing, I see myself stopping to check Facebook every so often (so very often) as I plod through hours of tedious editing. And I realize we are both a helpless mess, in need of grace.

"Therefore you have no excuse, O man, every one of you who judges. For in passing judgment on another you condemn yourself, because you, the judge, practice the very same things" (Rom. 2:1, ESV).

One evening I asked my challenge child to clear the dinner dishes from the table. Ten minutes later there she sat, engrossed in her latest *Magic Treehouse* book. She was oblivious to my request and the bits of turkey stuffing hardening on plates like barnacles on a wharf.

"You're done," I announced, dutifully snatching the paperback from her hand and disappearing into the living room to hide it. I returned to the kitchen and finished the dishes myself, aware that she needed no explanation for my action—and unaware that she was upstairs sobbing on her bed.

When I found her later, red-eyed and withdrawn, I realized it was time for a session in the green La-Z-Boy. I cradled her 'tween frame like a baby and, rocking, asked her what was wrong.

"You never listen to me either!" she burst into tears again.

Guilt gripped my throat. She was right. I'd become an expert (or so I thought) at feigning interest in her stories—a little nodding of the head and a few "mmms," "wows," "uh-huhs," and "ohs!" had bought me time as a listening impostor. Now the days of pretending were over.

"Sweetie, you are absolutely right. I am so sorry. I want to be a better listener. Can we make a deal to work on that with each other?" I held her close and kissed her wet cheeks as she agreed to our plan.

I admit I haven't always kept my part of the bargain. I still catch myself ignoring my children, and I have to ask them to repeat themselves. But that evening taught me that *I cannot expect from any one of my girls what I am unwilling to give to them myself.*

"Do not exasperate your children; instead, bring them up in the training and instruction of the Lord" (Eph. 6:4).

Learning to See

"I just seem to do all the wrong things! I don't mean to be a bad person, but I just can't help it." The scene is from *The Secret Life of Bees*, and the voice belongs to the character Lily. In a fit of tears the troubled girl has just told her guardian, August, that she is leaving home. She is the cause of everything that's gone wrong around her lately.[1]

I was awestruck by Lily and how much she reminded me of my most challenging child—everything about her, from her lanky figure to her long, blonde hair, blue eyes, and white skin; her adventurous spirit, love for nature, passion to help people and willingness to fight for them; her desire to write books; and the emotional outbursts (oh, those emotional outbursts!). I watched the girl on the screen with wonder as she endeared my heart to my daughter in a powerful way.

By the movie's end I was in tears and longing for the "Lily" living in my house. I dashed up the stairs to her bedroom, knelt beside her bed, and watched her sleep. How often did she feel the way Lily did—like a "bad person," the "difficult child"? Was she burdened by the feeling that she couldn't do anything right? That she would always be "in trouble"?

Was I the cause of those feelings? Was I pushing my daughter away—slowly out of the house—with my demands that she be other than herself? I desperately wanted it to not be true. I wanted her to stay close, forever.

I gazed at her, brushing wet hair away from her red, sweaty face. All at once I was reminded of everything I loved about my (then ten-year-old) daughter: her zest for life displayed in the way she skipped everywhere while others walked and the way she never stopped talking (and talking) about all she was reading and writing; her individualism—refusing pierced ears when all of her sisters had them; the way she could wear the same outfit all week and not care that she smelled like peanut butter and had to be peeled off of the dining room chair; her nonconformity and willingness to walk into the grocery store in her bathrobe and sneakers; her knack for instantly memorizing everything deemed worthy of memorizing (which, in her mind, was everything)—license plates, billboards, food labels, movie quotes, the exact location of Uzbekistan, and the hiding place for the Oreos that she (and always only she) discovered; how she chose to spend a Saturday learning Mandarin online while other kids played video games.

Even her annoying quirks were suddenly, strangely precious to me—her constant fidgeting and fiddling with things that seemed to topple over if she but looked at them; her rattling, high-pitched voice and throat that never seemed to need clearing; her eagerness to stamp-and-ink someone a card and press wild flowers into it; her frequent need to give a gift taken from the odds and ends of her under-the-bed stash of toiletries, crafts, and knickknacks; her love for God—her sincere, tender-hearted love for God, reflected in her devotion to the happiness of others.

How refreshing and wonderful it was to savor her uniqueness. I'd let things get in the way—namely, myself. After all, the things about her that drove me crazy were the very traits she inherited from me. I'd become too accustomed to living with a younger version of Faith. I needed to discover my unique, beautiful child.

I'm asking God to keep my vision clear, to help me always behold the beauty that makes my daughter the wondrous person she is—even when she "seems" to do the wrong things. I want my precious baby to always know she is *well loved*. I want to remind her of that every chance I get, even if it means holding tight around her rigid little frame until it softens by a mother's humble tears.

"How precious also are Your thoughts to me, O God! How vast is the sum of them!" (Ps. 139:17, NAS).

ADD Has Its Benefits

Current research shows individuals with attention deficit disorder (ADD) are advantageous in the workplace, so much so that some companies intentionally hire people with such a diagnosis. Parents can encourage children with ADD by pointing out their positive qualities and explaining how those qualities may contribute to the success of a company or organization someday. People with ADD tend to be:

- Empathetic
- Creative and ingenious
- Driven and enthusiastic
- "Hyperfocused" on a project until its completion, achievement-oriented
- Gifted with a great sense of humor
- Able to think outside the box
- Able to learn from difficulty

- **Highly intuitive**
- **Visionaries**
- **Able to see the bigger picture**
- **Able to thrive in chaotic situations**
- **Risk takers[2]**

 Refrigerator Magnet: Today I choose to appreciate and savor my child's uniqueness.

 Heart Exam: In what ways do I wrongly exact perfection from my child?

Chapter 6

TRYING TO BE
MISS EVERYTHING

FIVE YEARS AFTER I embarked on this book-writing adventure, I stepped away from it for a while. The unfinished manuscript occupied a shelf next to drawings of monsters and dot-to-dot printouts. I had taken some time off to grow up.

When I finally turned my attention back to writing, I knew I had grown up a little because when I left home to find a quiet a place to write, it hurt to drive away. As I kissed my angels' tousled hair and said good-bye, I wondered if they would survive without me. I knew they were in their daddy's good hands, but a part of me worried that I'd come home to find them malnourished, undereducated, filthy, corrupted by the media, living in a house unfit for human habitation, and suffering anxiety disorders from my twenty-four-hour absence.

I missed my children.

Don't dismiss me as being as extreme as the women I used to think were crazy because they couldn't leave their kids for a while. I assure you, I am normal. I relished the day's peace and coffee; I found enjoyment in the way my fingers tap-danced on the keyboard as though they hadn't for a long time. I didn't call home to find out if everyone was still alive. I was calm.

But forever embedded in my memory is the face of a little girl in the rearview mirror of my white Suburban. As tires rolled down the rocky driveway, she followed intently, taking her eyes off me for split-second intervals to watch her footing. I turned onto the dirt road, and she continued to follow, now running, barefoot, until I was out of sight. The expression on her face still haunts me; it was a look of despair at my being gone for a whole day.

I returned five minutes later to get my jacket. There was Ruthie, at the end of the driveway, as though she'd expected I'd be back that soon. As I greeted her through the driver window, I noticed a tear lingering beneath one eye. I had asked her not to cry when we said our good-byes (thus making it harder for me to leave). She had kept her promise, holding back a torrential downpour of emotion until I was gone.

My heart fluttered with revelation. Not only did I miss my children, but also they missed me. They *missed me!*

The next day I would walk through the front door and four chattering girls would attack me with hugs and reprimands for being gone so long. I looked forward to the reunion. That was strange. I used to want to run away forever.

Let's Make a Deal

Before I venture into the potentially dangerous territory of discussing "working moms," can we make a deal? If you work outside the home, I won't assume you're selfish or neglectful if you don't assume I'm a simpleton who forwent higher learning to raise bunnies—er, babies. Fair enough?

Let's lay aside prejudice and try to understand what may be behind why some women—inside or outside the home—tend to overwork or overdo. Face it; there are stay-at-home "Super Moms" who iron, bake, wax, and polish to the point of exhaustion and child neglect. And they are driven by the same things that drive many "working moms." We simply cannot judge what's going on in a person's heart on the basis of where she chooses to work.

This chapter is not about stay-at-home moms versus "working" moms. That would be unfair. There are moms who work outside the home because they are divinely called to do so and love their jobs. There are others who are financially unable to stay home. These words I write are my arms around *any otherwise frazzled and conflicted mother* and a whisper in her ear, saying, "We weren't meant to be this way."

"You're Gone Too Much!"

Every now and then I find myself engaged in a fascinating conversation with another mom that goes something like this:

Me: "So what have you been up to?"

Her: "Oh, it's crazy! I've just started night school, and I'm working weekends at the office. Jaden's in T-ball and Lacy's got tap dance recitals. Plus, we're all in Saturday's parade, and I'm designing the Girl Scout float. We're hosting Dave Ramsey classes, so that means I have to keep the house clean, which is hard because of the playroom construction. Oh, and I'm still directing the youth choir. Which reminds me, I have to price stuff for the church rummage sale tomorrow! And did I mention we just got a horse? Yeah, we're nuts. We don't sleep anymore, but it's all good!" she laughs.

That's when I become confused and wonder, "Does this person mean to complain—or brag? Is this array of activity meant to be a verbal display of insanity—or accomplishment? Am I to feel pity—or awe?"

Perhaps this woman's busyness is slightly exaggerated. Even so, is anything about her lifestyle familiar to you? Do you know this person? Does she live in your house?

I often ponder the heavy workloads and busy schedules of mothers who value a good night's sleep, mental and physical health, well-adjusted kids, and a hot love life, not to mention a thriving relationship with God. I wonder how many of us are allowing one or more of these to slip off a piled-high plate of activity. Many women, it seems, wear haggard expressions that testify to being overworked, overbooked, and overstressed. If it's not evidenced on their faces, it's often reflected, sadly, in their families.

I have been guilty. One time I noticed one of my daughters (guess who!) slipping into "impossible" mode. I donned my disciplinarian hat and banished her to her room to wait for me to cool down and come deliver her sentence (the usual decade-long grounding from books, sweets, and computer games). On my way upstairs I heard her sniffling. Something told me to shove my anger aside and listen. I asked her what was wrong and if I had anything to do with her behavior. After a few minutes of gentle coaxing, what finally came out was, "You're gone too much."

Ouch! I had not been available enough to give my

daughter the positive attention she needed; hence she was forced to vie for my attention her own way. I held her and apologized for my busyness and promised to start saying no to things. Her behavior turned around instantly. But saying no can be difficult. Why is that?

I think there are several reasons we sometimes put too much on our plates. I will spend the rest of this chapter discussing the first and, perhaps, most common reason. In the next chapter we'll dig deeper to explore other reasons. For now, will you be honest and ask yourself along with me: Why do we sometimes fall into the trap of needing to be Miss Everything?

Setting Priorities

For five years I served as a youth group leader. It didn't feel like "work": I loved my job so much, I didn't know when my workday began and ended. Twenty-four hours a day and seven days a week my mind was filled with event planning and texting Scripture messages to teens in need. The phone was never turned off; even family vacations didn't stop my constant attention to ministry.

My constant busyness caught up with me while I was attending a lakeside ladies' retreat. I sat zombie-like on the deck, so depleted of energy I was unable to play a simple board game with my friends. That weekend I heard a sermon in which the minister asked, "What banner hangs above your head?" Suddenly I saw myself driving a van with "Youth Ministry" in the proverbial front seat while my family was cooped up in the backseat yearning for the nurture I was giving to others. "Wife" and "Mother" were nowhere to be found on the banner of my life.

I took inventory on my four children: my daughter was to be married in a month; my oldest son was beginning college and struggling with choosing courses; my teenage son had just experienced a mild brush with the law; my youngest, like any ten-year-old boy, needed his mother's time and attention.

I met with my pastor and poured out my heart to him. Ministry had come before family for far too long. I left my post as youth leader and rediscovered my own little "flock." Today my husband is thrilled to have me to himself on Sunday evenings, and my daughter has cherished memories of her last month at home spent wedding planning with Mom. My sons are thriving. Circumstances eventually necessitated me finding a job and returning to a daily inspection of my priorities, but by God's grace I am determined to never leave my family in the backseat again.

—Kitty Ravert

A Crisis of Identity

A long time ago a friend eyed my blank calendar and teased, "You're such a homebody." Back then I wasn't sure whether to feel insulted or complimented. But today "Homebody" is my personal badge of honor. There is something beautiful about a woman—regardless of where she works—who is comfortable carrying the title "Mother." The woman who is 100 percent secure in God is OK with being "just a mom," if that is what He's called her to. Her identity is so intertwined with God's love that she can be "Homebody" or "Grass Stain Remover" and be more fulfilled than any prime time drama diva.

As I look around and see so many moms living on the brink of burnout, I can't help but wonder how many of them are trying to fulfill a calling that may be meant for later in life. How much of their identity and sense of self-worth is connected to a paycheck, a ministry, a volunteer position, a title, the applause of an audience, or letters behind their name?

Now, there's nothing inherently wrong with ambition. God places in us a desire to create more than just babies. We are made in His image. He is the Creator, the great Artist, and we are miniature masters of art. That is why I dream of one day hiding myself away in a quiet office and writing the books I carry in my heart. God does not give us these dreams only to snatch them away with the arrival of a family.

I used to have an inner fear that when my nest was finally empty, I'd be old and gray, too feeble to really "make something of myself." Then I met Thérèse Dion, mother of the famous singer Cèline Dion. Cèline was the fourteenth child and a most unwelcome "surprise." Mrs. Dion's youngest children, a set of twins, were getting ready to start school, and she was looking forward to the daytime empty nest. She'd been confined to the house for eighteen years and couldn't wait to gain her freedom, planning to work full-time in clothing retail. When Mrs. Dion discovered she was pregnant with Cèline, she despaired on the couch for a couple weeks. But eventually Mrs. Dion got to see more of the world through touring with her daughter than she ever dreamed!

I was intrigued with Mrs. Dion's story and went to meet her in her hometown of Charlemagne, Quebec. I found an eighty-two-year-old woman working full-time as the founder of an organization that provides school supplies to thousands of underprivileged kids in northeast Canada. Since her own children left home, she has launched a line of food products, run a catering business, hosted a cooking show, and toured the country speaking about health and nutrition. She told me she'd started her current occupation at age seventy-one and was nowhere near retiring. That's when I realized how silly and unrealistic my fear was. There are seasons to life; there is life after children!

I wonder if we humans, in an effort to make names for ourselves, either run after the wrong things or pursue the right things at the wrong time. I've done both.

For me, now is the time to embrace my children—completely. It is not a time to "juggle career and motherhood" or wear many hats. Mothering *is* my career. It's not a season for trying to hold it all together and hope my kids turn out OK. It's a moment that is all too fleeting and should be taken in as though deeply and slowly inhaling the fragrance of a freshly cut rose before its scent wears away.

Remember, it's not about *where* we work or *what* we do as much as *why* we do it. My sense of self-worth is tested each time I meet a sophisticated woman and she asks, "What do you do for a living?" I could rightly say, "I'm a writer," and feel pretty good about who I am. But why shouldn't I have the same satisfaction in declaring, "I'm a stay-at-home mom"?

Understand that I say this simply to affirm all mothers. We are not our work—housework or outside work. We are God's statement that the world needs nurturing by beautiful, relational beings called "women."

There was a day when all my focus was, sadly, on "becoming somebody"—on personal achievements and not on relationships with those I love most. I took my dad's earlier advice (in chapter 4) to mean only that I shouldn't be overly ambitious about what I can get done on a *daily* basis; I had failed to realize this applies to my whole life. I wasn't looking at the bigger picture.

Dad had said that life itself—not just each day—is about relationships. It's not about what you and I can accomplish. I am afraid that unchecked priorities or the premature pursuit of lofty dreams may weaken the bond a mother has between herself and her children, if not destroy it completely.

Speaking from personal past experience, a poor sense of self-worth is what drives some of us to be Miss Everything. And when we see others seemingly attaining to that status, the inevitable offshoot is a worse evil.

Envy

To quote my dad exactly: "The one thing in life that causes trouble and destruction on all levels is envy." When he first told me that, I blew it off as not being applicable to me or to anyone I knew, for that matter. I mean, who has a problem with envy? That's the vice exhibited by actors and politicians, not good little Christian mommies.

In his book *Envy: The Enemy Within*, Bob Sorge defines envy as "the [sometimes subtle] pain or distress we feel over another's success." He goes on to say that "envy's energies are generated from a self-seeking heart of personal ambition."[1] And misguided ambition, I might add, stems from a feeling of discontent with who we are.

Think about it. If I am truly content with who I am as a woman adored by God and created in His image, then feeling secure in my personal calling as a stay-at-home mom will follow. There'll be no need to run around like a headless chicken, trying to "find myself" in some new enterprise that takes over my life. Yet I used to sit at traffic lights and "direct" imaginary choirs as I listened to the Brooklyn Tabernacle Choir on CD—not for fun, but to torture myself with thoughts of how unfair it was that Carol Cymbala spent her days directing five hundred voices while I spent mine directing toddlers away from my freshly mopped floor.

And there was the day I turned on the radio to hear a mother of five being interviewed who had just launched a magazine while caring for a newborn at home and teaching at a university. I quickly tuned her out and decided I didn't like the woman at all and that she must be miserable because she surely doesn't have time, as I do, to crimp her daughter's hair or recline on the sofa with a good book and a cup of chai.

But I don't have a problem with envy.

Identity Crisis

If someone has a different career or ministry every time you see her, it could be evidence of an identity problem. For a season I believed I was destined to be a church pianist. I'd been at the forefront of music ministry where I attended Bible school and thought I was hot stuff on stage. One day in chapel I waxed eloquent from the pulpit: "If I never strike another key on the piano, strum another string on my guitar, or accomplish anything on this earth, let it be said in the end that I pleased God!" I pounded the podium for emphasis.

God heard those zealous words and put me to the test;

I got married and then got pregnant—four times! I left the piano bench and warmed a pew for the next decade, as baby after baby became my priority. My instruments rusted and fell out of tune from sitting untouched. I lost skill. I began having a recurring nightmare in which a cruel stretch of ebony and ivory drifted away from my frantic fingers every time I sat down to play.

My babies grew, and I found a place in the musical spotlight again. But something had changed. From the height of the platform I watched my family sing without me at their side. I longed to be with them. The thrill of public performance paled in the light of their faces. I handed in my lead sheets and joined Dave and the girls offstage for good.

Another time I was invited to be part of a newly formed drama team purposed to put on comedy plays for the community in a huge local theater. This was an invitation I couldn't pass up. I love to act, and the notion of playing a lead role before a large crowd was appealing. What's more, my kids were now old enough that attending rehearsals would not have put the same strain on my family that it would have in the days in which a baby was permanently affixed to my breast. With hubby's blessing, "Homebody" left home and eagerly headed for stardom.

The first script-reading session was exhilarating. I enjoyed throwing myself into various characters as though trying on cocktail dresses of every style and color for an entire evening. For two whole hours I was not "Mom." I was "Miss Hollywood." Look out, world!

But shortly after that first drama team meeting something strange happened. As I looked at the calendar and filled in the dates for upcoming practices, I no longer felt excited. I actually yawned. Before I knew it, I was calling to let the team leader know I wouldn't be part of the drama club after all.

I'll never forget the moments after I made that phone call. I was sitting on my bed, letting it sink in that I had just turned down an opportunity I had dreamed of for years—becoming "famous" on stage. My lips curled into a smile and a chuckle escaped from within me. Once again I didn't need to "be somebody." It was because I finally knew I already was.

Longing for the Spotlight

As I flip through my journals, I feel a sense of shame at the shallowness of what I was wanting out of life only a few years ago. My prayers were requests for some place in the spotlight—anywhere I could have a following of people besides my children. I was consumed with lust for recognition and bothered especially by mothers my age who were finding themselves on a public pedestal. Somehow the world would discover Faith.

For a while I had a Friday morning radio spot on a local station in which for five minutes my pearls of wisdom were broadcast to whoever happened to be listening. But I fell into this recurring scenario: I'd rush the girls through the bedtime routine, grab Ruthie, sit in the rocker, and rock back and forth at almost vibrating speed (it's amazing how fast you can make a rocking chair go!). I'd sing "Jesus Loves Me" to the beat of the frantic rocking; then hastily tuck her in bed and say, through gritted teeth, "Now you *stay there*! I've got a radio broadcast to record."

Two minutes later I'd be at my laptop announcing into the microphone through a forced smile, "Hi, I'm Faith Bogdan with a 'Momspiration'—a word to inspire you toward better mothering." Something was terribly wrong with that picture.

Eventually I found myself at a writer's conference browsing the book table. Some colorful greeting cards were on display, and one in particular jumped out at me. It read, "You were handpicked by God to share your faith with a captivated audience." The assertion tickled my ego. A confirmation! I was made for greatness.

Neglecting to notice the A-B-C blocks pictured on the front, I flipped the card open and read the inside: "You are doing a wonderful job of lovingly shaping the life of your little one."[2] My face went hot as I realized I'd grossly misinterpreted the card's message.

Katie Luce, wife of nationally known youth minister Ron Luce, had a similar epiphany once. While on a ministry road trip with a crowd of young people, her baby, Hannah, cried for almost the whole trip. Kate looked at her daughter and thought, "You are ruining my ministry." That's when she heard God's gentle reprimand: *"She* is your ministry."[3]

Free to Be Me

I was at prayer one evening and felt the distinct impression that God was asking me the same question He once asked King Solomon: "What do you want out of this life more than anything else?"

I mentally reviewed all the things I dreamed of doing and becoming. I had begun to accept the fact that I was not likely to see those dreams become a reality until my last child left for college in about forty years.

As I pondered how I should answer God's question, I realized it would be a shame to attain to those heights of success if it meant ending up with children who didn't love God or who wouldn't want to come to visit me or take care of me, if need be, in my old age. How tragic it would be to lose them in any way, shape, or form because of my misplaced priorities. So I answered thus: "I would really like to love my children completely, whatever the cost."

God answered my prayer by a process Bob Sorge describes as "weaning." He says that "God withholds what we want in order to change our desires,"[4] and the green-eyed monster is dealt with in the process. If someone has something I no longer want, there's no reason to envy her. By using the care of my children to prevent me from following selfish ambition, God is removing prestige-chasing and power-hunger from my heart. He is replacing it with a boundless enjoyment of motherhood and a deep sense of fulfillment that keeps my heart bonded to the doorpost of my home.

I cannot begin to express how freeing it is to be truly happy for someone who has or achieves something *right for her* but what I no longer need for my own identity. It is simply amazing to discover that, even with the prospect of writing books, it doesn't matter to me any more—as far as fame and fortune go—whether my name will make it to the best-seller list. Gone are the days of wishing, hoping, dreaming, and pining for fame.

This is what I wrote in my journal just a few years ago:

I have finally "woken up and smelled the children." It took eight years. I have fully embraced not just motherhood but *them*. I've made peace with my dirty house and neglected projects. I've put my book ideas and articles safely away, locked in a "future" box. I am enjoying my kids and rapidly witnessing the ever-increasing fruits of selfless labor. The character I see developing in Anna, Sarah, Rebecca, and Ruthie makes losing my life to save theirs well worth it.

♡♡♡

I once watched a video of best-selling author Ann Voskamp being interviewed on stage at Patrick Henry College. During the question-and-answer session a woman in the audience complimented her book and then asked her, "What is the Lord speaking to you right now? What is He working in your heart?" (In other words, "What exciting new book are you working on? To what new heights is your writing and speaking career taking you?")

Ann hesitated, and her chin began to quiver. Then she choked out these words: "Honestly, in this particular season of my life, I have never felt more committed to motherhood and the eternal value of children. My life right now…doesn't look like I want it to look. I want to be home with my kids this morning.…Because, ultimately, how those six children walk with the Lord means more to me than anything else."[5]

I thought, "Yes! Someone gets it!" I wanted to reach through the screen and hug her.

There was a day when I was consumed with getting my kids grown and out of the house so I could make a name for myself. Today the only limelight I need is the light in my children's eyes as they respond to being loved twenty-four hours a day, seven days a week. It's an amazing, wonderful, and surprising place for me to *find myself.*

 Refrigerator Magnet: The woman who knows she's well loved by God has no reason to envy others.

 Heart Exam: Where does my identity come from?

Chapter 7

OTHER REASONS WE DO TOO MUCH

Hear my heart on this matter: *I care about moms.* Too many of us live on the verge of burnout and physical breakdown, doing the things we think we have to do. It's time to step off this ride. Perhaps we can look deeper within our hearts and find out whether there are other hidden motives for dragging our tired bones from place to place or project to project, sometimes doing what we don't even like to do.

So far I've suggested that much of our hyperactivity has to do with a need to prove ourselves—a lack of contentment with who we are. Now I'd like to explore five more areas that sometimes shove us into Miss Everything's trap. I have been guilty on at least two counts! How about you?

Pleasers

Oprah calls it the "Disease to Please." Joyce Meyer refers to it as "Approval Addiction." You know her—the woman who needs a bumper sticker that says, "You can't please everybody, but it sure is worth a try." That poor soul apparently does think it's worth trying to do the impossible. Otherwise she would simply say, "No."

Such is the "Super Mom" I described in the previous chapter. Part of the reason she's about to lose her marriage and her child is becoming more and more unmanageable is that she is a bona fide people pleaser. Unfortunately those she would please the most are not living under her roof. In many cases they are unrelated and hardly known. Yet they remain the glad benefactors of her tireless service. They will pay her in "atta girls" and thumbs-ups, and the emotional buzz from that affirmation will last only until she's asked to give again.

It saddens me that we can be so exhaustingly enslaved to the good opinions of those who ask our favors. For some of us, the fear of disapproval is so great that it's worth trading in our sanity, health, and family relationships in order to stay in the public's good graces.

Why is this? I believe it is, again, linked to identity. Show me a person who is not secure in who God says she is, and I'll show you a woman marked by the need to be liked by everyone. As I've already described, this can manifest as selfish ambition ("everyone will like me if I'm rich and famous"). But in the present case the same image problem can show itself in endless ill-motivated servitude ("everyone will like me if I give and give some more"). This is, in fact, another type of self-centered behavior.

Praise junkies are driven by a deceptive inner voice that constantly hisses, "Don't disssappoint them! They'll like you lessssssss!" As one who thrives on words of affirmation, I am well attuned to that voice. But I'm learning to close my ears since I started observing how utterly destructive the disease to please is on so many levels. If saying yes to leading the community development team means giving up much-needed talk time with my husband or play dates with my children, forget it. Upon declining my services I silently chant my favorite mantra: "The world won't end and no one will die if I say no."

But again, saying no can be hard. Whether it's small scale, as in being asked to volunteer, or on a bigger scale, affecting lifelong decisions, we often can't bear to disappoint. I saw this illustrated once when a young mom tearfully confessed to me that she was agonizing her days away in beauty school, feeling pressured by her family to get a "real job" while a sitter raised her son. She didn't want to do hair (and it would have been fine if she did); she wanted to be home with her little boy. But the need to please was strong enough to have sway on her career.

Friends, I am imploring us all once again to find our self-worth in God and hang what people think—yes, even those close to us. At the end of our lives it's God we'll answer to, and it's our children we'll want by our side at heaven's gate.

Woman Power

Sometimes our priorities get displaced because of feminism gone awry. There are mothers who feel a need to convince society that they can do what a man can do. So they throw the kids in day care and go off to engineering school, all the while blubbering about how they miss being at home.

I'm not sure they're proving anything we don't already know. If I wanted to design aircraft, I would have signed up for it. But I get more satisfaction out of designing good character in my kids. I am not threatened by anyone—male or female—who would wrongly assume that's "all I'm capable of."

It seems to me the more certain one is about something, the less she has to prove it to be true. I'm pretty secure in knowing that Donald Trump could not afford to pay me for what I do. So I'll gladly stay home (or work at a job I love) rather than go out frantically waving the "I'm-your-equal" banner in men's faces every day.

Now, you may feel a call to do roadside construction work or arrest crackheads in dark alleys. Great! Enjoy it. I have girlfriends who take welding classes and know how to use a table saw. They do those things because they love them and have a genuine interest in learning those trades. I have mom-cop friends and she-engineer friends, sensei friends and girlfriends who know where to find the radiator and how to change a spark plug, doctor-friends whose husbands stay at home with the kids part-time so they can see patients, and friends who make their livings by shoving arms up the back ends of cows. I applaud them for following their passions and putting their talents to use. As a matter of fact, I believe I have two budding female scientists under my roof at this very moment.

But I know for a fact that there are other women who take on certain jobs for the sole purpose of trying to be the "son" their father never had or the kind of woman they think a postmodern society expects them to be. I've talked with them and witnessed their conflicted tears. Friends, this is sad. If your heart says, "Stay home, breastfeed, and crochet," and you are financially able, do it with all your girl power and might, and do it proudly.

Experts

Indeed, the world won't end if you say no. But it may feel that way if you relinquish control of something to someone who doesn't do it quite as well as you do. If you don't head up that school board project again this year, a part of you will suffer. It's the part that knows you're the most qualified to do it. A program may fall apart without your skill and expertise. At best it may be a close-to-worthless operation in your absence. Saying no to an area of service that has always been your "baby" will cause you grief. Go ahead and cry it out. Mourn the loss of self. Sing the song "Anything [They] Can Do I Can Do Better" for the last time. Then suck it up and go love your family. Because the truth is, that's where you'll end up the happiest. After all, no one does *that* quite like you either.

Stuff

Last night I had a dream. It was a romantic dream, the kind that leaves one floating and fanciful all day, still ravished by the night's sweet memories. I dreamed of a past love.

When I could stand it no longer, I told my husband. It was only right that he know what feelings were enrapturing me during innocent sleep. I knew he would understand and offer sympathy for my unintended visitation to a seductive past. You see, I dreamed I had gone shoe shopping.

Famous Brands in Watkins Glen was having an end-of-the-season clearance sale on Birkenstock sandals. There was a pair for Sarah in a size 5 of blue floral corduroy, closed toe, ankle strap. They were only $3.99. So were the pink ones for Ruthie and the black ones for Rebecca. It still pains me that it was only a dream.

And it will remain so, for at the time of this writing my fresh-out-of-grad-school husband is one of the many victims of the current recession. As he seeks elusive employment, we are surviving—no, thriving—on faith and venison.

I have found that I can live a happy and fulfilled life without Kleenex and dinner napkins. And who knows what goes on in restaurant kitchens anyway? I am using the same coffee maker that was given to us as a wedding present nineteen years ago. We still have a box-shaped TV, and I don't own a cell phone. My wardrobe is mostly secondhand.

Eighty-seven-cent VO5 shampoo cleans my hair just fine, and I won't die without an iPad. We still camp in the same tent we bought ten years ago; two of its door zippers are pinned together, but it keeps us dry. In my home a white toilet is situated dutifully next to a chocolate-brown sink. I outgrew my need for matching dishes and silverware long ago. The kitchen appliances are a mix of chrome, black, and white. The eighties-blue Formica is buckling and the linoleum is peeling up along the edges and seams.

But the guests always want to come back. Dave keeps coming back, in a car you can hear from a mile away.

We don't need more "stuff" to make us happy. There was a day when I didn't think twice about whipping out a twenty-dollar bill to sport a new bracelet or pair of earrings. But neither did I give second thought to a neighbor in need. For me, traveling the road to compassion required walking in the shoes of the desolate. On the way I found contentment. I am both poorer and happier than I have ever been.

If you feel conflicted between working for the sole purpose of "having more" and wanting to be at home, I can tell you that I would give up our second car and eat beans and rice before I would go to work. My mother felt the same way when I was a kid. I wore hand-me-downs and played with used toys. We didn't have money for team sports or vacations, but I still thought I was the luckiest kid in the world. I had no idea how financially strapped my parents were until I learned of it as an adult.

"Oh, but I want my little Chadwick to have it better than I did," you might say. If that is true, spend more time with him. That's all he really wants. Kids are as well off as we tell them they are by our availability and involvement.

One afternoon I was enjoying a hike along our nature trail with Ruthie. Five-year-old Ruthie, who had never played the Wii. Ruthie, who had been to the movie theater once and had eaten only one Happy Meal in her life. Ruthie, who rode a used, rusty tricycle and *will not* own an iPhone when she's ten! Trees of every kind towered over us in full spring foliage, creating a lush green archway through which to walk.

"Do we own all this land, Mom?" Ruthie spun around with her arm outstretched, pointing to woods in every direction.

"All that you see, my dear."

"Wow. We're *rich!*" she announced, and skipped down the path ahead of me.

I chuckled to myself. "I suppose we are."

From Engineer to Stay-at-Home Mom

Out of college I was blessed with my dream job in Mission Control Center as a flight control engineer for NASA. During shuttle missions, when astronauts said, "Houston, we have a problem," our team launched into action to develop unique solutions for those issues. In 1995 I was fortunate to be one of five people that NASA sent to Gagarin Cosmonaut Training Center, or "Star City," in Russia when an American astronaut flew onboard the Russian space station Mir.

Fast forward through marriage, our first child, and the decision to become a stay-at-home mom. "NASA engineer," no problem. "Great mom," yikes! There was no training, no mommy checklist, and no flight control team to help me make decisions. At home I felt isolated and lonely because my friends were still at NASA. For the first time in my life I didn't know what to do.

Over time God revealed to me that I didn't need my job to feel secure, because I am His—first and foremost. I learned that if I follow Him, while doing my part to remain strong in body and mind, I can walk through my parenting job with confidence to shape a Christ-based home and family.

Mission Control Center gave me tools to make strong, swift decisions—tools I now use at home. I know that being a mom is the most significant career that I will ever have because of the eternal impact it has on future generations. That knowledge fills me with peace and purpose that far exceed the thrill of working at NASA. Now when I hear, "Mommy, we have a problem," I smile and give thanks for the opportunity to invest in my family.

—Kristen Taraszewski

"It's All About the Kids"

I was heart-broken for Jon and Kate Gosselin (of the 2009 reality TV series *Jon & Kate Plus 8*). A marriage breakdown is bad enough. But to have the world photograph and gloat over your breakup must make for a miserable life. I don't care how big their house was.

During one television interview Jon poured out his frustrations over the ever-present paparazzi and other things related to parenting eight children in a fish bowl. I wanted it to be over, just as he did. So my ears perked up when he started talking about ending the TV series. My hope was short-lived though. For what he said, in essence, was that he and Kate would stop doing the show when their kids said they didn't want to do it anymore.

Their *kids*? I couldn't believe what I was hearing. The ruling multiples would determine their parents' vocation. How often is this scenario repeated in families across America? Thrones of homes are occupied by diapered kings—demanding toys, activities, and programs they neither need nor really want.

And the parents are suckered by it. Wanting to give their children opportunities they didn't have, they work long hours, often far away from home, to satisfy not only little King Jayden but also some inner need of their own. Maybe I am wrong, but I can't help but wonder if some of the parents of child-centered homes were raised by mothers who didn't find much fulfillment in being a mom.

I once overheard an interesting conversation between a woman and her young daughter. The girl had been saying things such as, "You don't love me" and, "I wish I hadn't been born." Trying to prove otherwise, the mother reminded her daughter of all their exotic travels, her fancy toys, and endless extracurricular activities in which she was involved. "You see? I love you. That's why I make sure you have all the things I never had."

I felt for the girl. I had to wonder if her mother had asked her what would really make her feel loved, whether she might have answered, "To play catch out back with you," or "To make play dough together." I suspected that mom could only give to her daughter what her mother had given to her: substitutes for what the child needed most—her mother's undivided attention.

Another time I watched a mother drag her five-year-old to cheerleading practice after the little girl had been nodding off to sleep at the dinner table. The child had been having behavioral problems—biting other kids and telling her mother what a mean mom she was. I wondered how things might have changed for the better if "Lila" had been allowed to snuggle up with Mom and a storybook that evening before being tucked into bed. (The girl had confided in me that she didn't really enjoy cheerleading!) Somehow I had the feeling that her parents were more interested in doing what they felt an all-American family is "supposed to do" rather than doing what was best for their child.

Some women seek to fulfill their own dreams through their offspring. So they put their kids into every after-school club and make them perform to the point of exhaustion. They don't realize that through emphasizing so much "doing" rather than "being," they are passing on an ambition-driven way of life that will continue to successive generations until someone wisely breaks the cycle.

I am not against extracurricular activities altogether, especially if they serve the purpose of tapping into a child's potential. Sarah is currently attending a young writer's critique group every other week. It's a half-hour drive, and gasoline costs almost the same as a mortgage payment, but those car rides provide precious one-on-one time with her. I cherish those trips and conversations we have about her writing future.

Anna spent a week living on the campus of Ithaca College last summer, attending a hands-on health care exploration camp. (She was only fourteen, the youngest among a large group of high school juniors and seniors. I meant to send her to a day camp at a local hospital lasting only three days but accidentally filled out the wrong online form and shipped my little girl away to college. I don't want to hear a word about it; she loved it and I survived.) She also plays in a jazz band at a local high school once per week.

Ruthie and Rebecca (now nine and ten) have yet to be involved in any extracurricular activity, unless you count homemade piano lessons, which consist of me stirring something at the stove and hollering for the nearby Yamaha Clavinova to please play in the right key. I'm sure they'd much rather take tumbling or ballet, but I don't have the money for that right now, and I'm quite happy to have that excuse. I refuse to wear us out by always being on the go, especially for involvement in things that won't matter so much *for them* in the long run. (Besides, ballet causes bunions. Who wants bunions?) If you're like me, and dance or team sports just isn't an option, let me reassure you that your kids will still thrive. I never had any of those things growing up and yet have very happy childhood memories.

Do you want to know what kind of memories my kids are going to have? We made a special one just recently. The girls are interested in medieval times, so we made a whole Saturday of it. We brought a tray full of snacks to the family room, turned off the lights, and lit candles everywhere. Then we snuggled on the couch and watched a long documentary on the Dark Ages. The girls were spellbound. Call us nerds, but now my kids know the difference between a Viking and a knight and what the Crusades were all about. It seemed we learned more in that one afternoon than I learned in my whole public school history class experience (but that's another matter!). The point is, we had fun and made a lasting memory together, and it didn't cost a dime or wear us thin. I love my homebody life!

And yet I understand that we are all in different places and our motherhood journeys won't look the same. There are moms who have reason to busy themselves for a season: soldier moms, widowed moms, and moms who are lonely for other reasons. (These are all good reasons for the rest of us to break out of our bubble and touch the world every now and then!) There are women who are wired in such a way that they can be constantly running to and fro and never miss a beat. They hire housecleaners, need less sleep, and don't mind a baby wrapped around their torso as they hustle from one place to the other. Some moms' jobs or hobbies are conducive to having kids in tow. Other moms have a half-dozen fewer kids than the rest of us, which makes these things easier. Still others hate to be at home as much as I love to, and their kids are turning out just fine.

Again, my intent here is not to pass a blanket judgment on moms who live out of a minivan. I am simply asking those of us who feel like we are falling apart to take a step back and try to see what may be obvious to others. Ask yourself, "*Why* am I doing so much?"

The Heart of the Matter

I subtitled this section "It's All About the Kids" because that is certainly what it appears to be in many homes. We want to believe that we work hard and keep demanding schedules solely for the sake of our children. For those who have a high-stress lifestyle and believe it is exclusively for the betterment of your kids, may I gently suggest taking an honest look within yourself to see if that is really the case? Is running to and fro "to please Johnny" instead more about you—your image as an "involved" mother, your fear that Johnny won't love you if you say "not today" or "not this year" or "not this toy"? Is it your desire to make him a "Junior Everything," a reflection of who you think the world wants you to be?

It has been said that "the heart of the matter is the matter of the heart." We can't see into each other's hearts, but we can each look deep into our own. I have a feeling that someone reading this—at least *one* dear mother—is going to do that and realize, "You know what? I can't find one good reason for running myself ragged like this." If that is you, I am saying, along with all my fellow home-bodies and homebodies-at-heart, it's quite all right if you want to resign as Miss Everything.

If you are a woman of faith, let me tell you about an exciting job opportunity. It is a distinguished ambassador position, one of highest rank, involving a specified mission. The benefits outweigh any six-figure salary it could ever pay. The amazing thing is, no experience or education is necessary! The only requirement is your availability.

The incumbent will be appointed as representative of the highest government in the universe. She will maintain solid relations with those to whom she is sent and engage in important discussions about the kingdom she represents. She is authorized as a personal messenger from the King of her eternal homeland.

Yes, God would appoint you, Mom, as His heavenly ambassador to your children. He has reviewed the potential candidates for this assignment and finds you—*you*—the most qualified for the task.

Are you interested in becoming the director of your child's eternal destination? Making God-lovers out of those entrusted to your care will be your chief enterprise. There is satisfaction to be found in merely being a mom. But to become Ambassador Mom—that is a title that knows no boundaries of pleasure and fulfillment.

Refrigerator Magnet: No one could afford to pay me for what I do.

 Heart Exam: Am I too busy to effectively be "Ambassador Mom" to my kids? If so, what is at the root of my busyness?

Chapter 8

WHO'S AT THE CENTER
OF YOUR HOME?

L ET'S GET A couple of things straight before you proceed to read this and the following chapter:

1. *I am human.* I'm prone to error and limited in my understanding of a lot of things—life in general, yours in particular. In fact, I am quite possibly the most ignorant person you will ever meet. I may even be a bit insane. I may say some things in the following pages that scream of idiocy. If you feel that is the case, I humbly ask you to cut me some slack and pretend this and the next chapter didn't happen.

2. *I like to think that I am full of grace.* I'm allergic to judgmentalism. I hate it. So if anything I write (or have written) smells of self-righteousness, please understand that is not my intent. As I said before, *I care.* This book—flawed as it may be—is my feeble attempt to help mothers and save the children.

Lions and Tigers in Bed, Oh, My!

No sooner had I become a mother than the first in a perpetual line of advice-givers approached me and gushed, "I've got *just* the book for you to read! It's called *The Family Bed.*" With all due respect, I am sure the author's kids turned out just fine. I imagine they each grew up to turn their own king-sized beds into dens and are living happily-ever-sexless-after.

Now, if you sleep curled around a munchkin or two and it doesn't interfere with certain aspects of your life (namely—sleep, sex, and the safety of your children), don't let me or anyone else make you feel bad about it. There is a time and place for "the family bed." This is not black and white. I fully understand we have our unique circumstances. There are reasons people adopt nontraditional sleeping arrangements: bad mattresses and bad backs; small living spaces; single, military, and widowed moms; third world moms in one-room huts; and married American mothers who have figured out how to make this work.

My own sister is a groovy, hippie-type mom who does some things differently than I do, and you know what? "Amazing Grace" is raising incredibly great, well-adjusted, and well-behaved kids. So I'm not here to judge or write the rules. And I would never want to categorize or label moms in a way that suggests one method is right and another is wrong. At any given moment my life situation could change and give me reason to haul my kids into bed with me.

But if I may, I'd like to propose the idea of "the marriage

bed" to those who may be interested. What this means is that, for example, Dave and I share a room and bed together *alone*. That doesn't mean Rebecca can't come snuggle with me in the night after a bad dream or that Ruthie and I don't enjoy early morning cuddles under warm blankets. I relish those moments and cherish memories of snuggling in bed with my own mom in the mornings, the two of us yawning like roaring lions together. But for Dave and me, where we sleep is sacred, because it is also where we...well, I'll get to that. (I have always wondered how that works for couples of "the family bed." It obviously worked somehow!)

The book *On Becoming Baby Wise* offers some compelling reasons to consider trading in the family bed for the marriage bed. I don't agree with everything in the book and am not necessarily recommending it, but the author makes some points about bed sharing that I would like to share with you here:

1. The American Academy of Pediatrics, as well as the majority of American health care professionals, agrees that bed sharing increases the risk of SIDS and death by suffocation.

2. It disrupts the child's sleep patterns.

3. It encourages separation anxiety.

4. It does not foster trust (which should be based on the parent/child relationship and not on the child's proximity to the parent).

5. It is a natural contraceptive (which may not always be a good thing).

6. And my personal favorite, as if the obvious needs to be stated: "It is well documented that the more people there are in a bed, the less soundly parents will sleep." —Dr. Richard Ferber[1]

Please understand I am addressing this section specifically to those who feel resentful about the invasion of little people in their bed and have the means to fix it. You're tired of small heads bobbing up to see what's going on beneath the sheets. I am here to "give you permission," if you will, to reclaim "the marriage bed" without guilt. If that's impossible due to a child who refuses to retire in his own bed, stay with me as I discuss discipline in the next chapter.

Men and "Golf"

Not every home has a literal "family bed," but some moms have a "family bed" approach to marriage. What I mean is, the kids and other things take priority in gigantic proportion over the husband-wife relationship. Consequently their husbands suffer a serious lack of uh..."golf." That's right, golf.

See, God wired men to really need to play a lot of golf. I don't know why, except that if it weren't this way, the world would be gravely underpopulated, because women don't seem to have as frequent a desire to hit the golf course. (Bear with me. My mother is going to read this book!)

I had been married for at least ten years before it sunk

into my thick head that husbands require a vastly higher level of "bedroom maintenance" than wives. I knew they liked to play golf more often; I even knew they needed it. But I thought they needed it like I need dark chocolate, when, in fact, they need it like I need a drink of water when I'm thirsty. And it's not just because of their hormonal makeup. There are two important reasons we wives should say yes to golf more often:

1. It makes our husbands feel loved in the same way conversation and cuddling make us feel loved.

2. It makes our husbands feel loved in the same way conversation and cuddling make us feel loved.

That was not a misprint. The next time you feel emotionally distant from your man, try this shortcut to getting that "in-love" feeling back: take off your nursing bra and "just do it."

"Marriage is not a place to 'stand up for your rights.' Marriage is a decision to serve the other, whether in bed or out" (1 Cor. 7:4, The Message). Too often moms refuse to play golf. We say we'd love to, even that we miss the sport, but we're too tired or busy to take it up any more. We have kids to bathe, kids to put to bed, online stuff to buy, dogs to groom, floors to mop, costumes to sew, blogs to write, office hours to keep, chats to finish, games to play, and sleep to get. So we drag our flannel-gowned selves into bed late at night, and there he lies with that silly grin, expecting us to pack our bags and go play golf.

Right, we think, and turn our backs on our husbands and fall asleep, feeling justified.

Excuses

But are we justified? Let's think about some of the things that keep us "off the golf course" with our mates. For example, do you feel you're not "mom enough" if you don't bathe your slippery newborn in a sudsy tub every day? Are daily baths for all of your children a part of your nighttime drill—making you more of a sergeant than a sleep fairy? I'm going to tell you something that might cause you to breathe a sigh of relief (after getting over your shock) and hang the washcloth out to dry: current research shows that our Western obsession with cleanliness has given rise to eczema as well as compromised our immune systems. Daily scrubbing damages the protective layer of the skin, drying it out and messing with those friendly little bacteria that live there and keep us healthy.[2]

So if you ask me, I'd say as long as you can still recognize your child and can't smell him coming, leave off with the hyper hygiene. Keep your newborn's face washed smooth and pimple-free, his bottom scrubbed stink-free, and the folds of the neck and the area behind the ears scoured of Limburger cheese out of consideration for his social life. Put the bubble bath in its proper place— a special "Mommy ritual" once or twice a week. In our house those who are still years away from puberty take Saturday baths. The older girls don't take baths at all; they take showers. Long showers. Why'd-you-lock-this-door-I-have-to-pee long showers. But I digress.

Pets sometimes paw their way into a marriage and

cause undue stress, thus hindering romance. I loved our old black mutt, Domino, who is buried outside the window where I write. He was an easy dog and minded his own business. I personally don't need my own version of Beethoven slobbering and shedding all over the house, giving me reason to stay up too late, tending to other than spouse. (I did not mean for that to rhyme.) I know a couple who separated over nine cats in the bedroom; I guess they practiced what you'd call "the pet bed."

How about this one: Does the kitchen have to be spotless before you retire for the night? There was a time I couldn't go to bed with dishes in the sink. If I was out for the evening, I expected Dave to do the dishes. If I came home to find pots and pans piled high on the countertops, I'd fume, slam things around, and say, "Don't expect anything from *me* tonight!" But by then, why would he *want* anything?

I wised up and started training myself to compartmentalize and head upstairs to bed without the awareness that my kitchen even existed. It no longer mattered whether the stainless steel in my sink greeted me next morning with a shine or not.

Not that Dave never does dishes. Actually, he's the master of a vacuum, broom, and dishcloth. I've told husbands who aren't clued in to the benefits of helping their wives around the house, "Dave gets anything he wants from me." (He is suddenly choking, watching me type these words.) But I also needed to lower my expectations—of Dave and of always having a spotless house.

But He Won't Talk to Me!

You may say, "That's great for you, Faith. But my situation is different. My husband won't talk to me. I'm not about to strip for someone who neglects me emotionally." I understand. This section is geared toward the mom who sees the need for improvement in an otherwise stable marriage. But there are complicated situations involving infidelity, pornography, and other difficulties to which my words will not apply. If that is you, I'd reach through this page and give you a hug if I could. Far be it from me to pretend all marriage problems are so simple.

But I can empathize to a degree with an uncommunicative husband. In our early years of marriage there was a metaphorical place known as "the Dave Cave" to which Dave retreated on a regular basis. He'd stay there for about three days, completely shut down, virtually ignoring me. I knew it was because he was "frustrated," and I knew the only way to get him out of the cave was to "play golf." And I resented it. I resented being the one to have to break the vicious cycle. If he would simply *talk* to me, I'd *want* to hit the green! But he wasn't talking. So I'd take my imaginary "rope" (sex) and yank him out of the cave.

But that didn't keep him from retreating further into the cave. The permanent barring of the Dave Cave, for me, was realizing what sent him there in the first place. It was usually one of two things:

Nagging

An incident occurred during the first year of our marriage in which I had been nagging Dave to fix something. We had climbed into bed for the night, and the faucet of my mouth was still dripping. Suddenly I noticed tears running down Dave's face as he lay there next to me. I was shocked. My big, strong outdoorsman was crying! I had never seen such a thing.

"What's wrong?" I asked, quickly turning off the faucet.

"Please. Don't. Nag. Me," he said, quietly. He went on to explain that he had once vowed he'd never have a nagging wife. "Ugh," I thought. "I once vowed I'd never be that kind of wife!" That incident all but cured my nagging. I have my relapses, but Dave would tell you I'm much improved compared to how I used to be. (I ask him!)

"It's better to live alone in the corner of an attic than with a quarrelsome wife in a lovely home" (Prov. 25:24, NLT).

Physical neglect

I had to start seeing Dave as a machine that would only operate smoothly as long as it was maintained properly. Not that sex became mechanical at all. It's just that I needed to place importance on it as one would carefully see to it that her car has enough oil and so on. *I count it an extreme privilege to be the only human being on the face of the earth literally certified to meet my husband's sexual needs.*

I sought—and found—joy in making love frequently. Yes, when the kids were small and I was exhausted, it seemed more like I'd signed up for "Zombie Zumba." But the reward was immediate—a supremely happy husband snuggling close to me in bed, his cup of love filled up and overflowing into my thirsty-for-love heart.

Of course, Dave had his part to play. Like many men, he needed to master the art of conversation. His lack of understanding my need sent me into my own sort of cave. Only for me it wasn't a quiet retreat. It was more like standing at the cave's entrance, screaming, "If you don't talk to me, I'm going to run and be gone from you forever!" So we went to a Marriage Encounter weekend, and he learned to talk to me.[3]

Fourteen years since that retreat, he has more than learned to communicate. After dinner he'll call to me from the couch and say, "Come digest [relax and talk] with me." Now I'm the one who has to make a conscious effort to walk away from what I'm doing and converse with my man. My husband loves to talk! There is hope for others.

Marriage Is Worth Fighting For

Whatever issues may have caused an emotional barbed-wire fence to divide your marriage bed in half, I encourage you to get help. Go to counseling. If your husband isn't keen on the idea, get keen on his eyeballs. Look at him intently and say something like, "Honey, I understand your need for more love-making. And I'm working on that. But I need you to understand that my level of need for conversation is equivalent."

One night I had a heart-to-heart with Dave about the distance I felt forming between us. I did this at a time when his belly was full of good food, he wasn't stressed out, all media distraction was turned off, and the kids were in bed. (Timing is everything when it comes to bringing up sensitive issues!) I looked him tenderly in the eyes and reminded him that when people don't get their needs for communication met within their marriage, they often seek to satisfy that desire for relationship elsewhere. I told him the last thing I wanted was for anything to weaken or destroy our marriage, but we had to be proactive to keep our relationship strong. He listened.

More than once I have turned on the lamp over Dave's head after he'd rolled over to go to sleep at night, getting in his face and explaining that our marriage had to be more important than anything else. I know my husband and what I can get away with. His humble personality lends itself to being able to receive this kind of communication. And he did. He *got it.*

I am by no means suggesting all wives should use the same tactic. Some women might be thrown out of the house and have the door slammed in their face if they tried this. Or else it might make no difference at all. But again, it is often not about the words we say as much as how we say them. I was prayed up and very careful about how I said these things to Dave.

I think if things had turned out differently and Dave showed no signs of change, I may have said something like, "Do you care to save our marriage and family?" (Again, this is not to be an off-the-cuff question spoken as you pull up to the ATM machine or drive to church. We wives can learn a thing or two about timing and sensitivity in communication. I used to think that dining out was the perfect opportunity to bring up heavy topics, but I quickly learned that a man just wants to enjoy his steak!)

If Dave had said he did want to save our marriage and family, I'd have taken that as a green light to insist on going to counseling. If he wanted to keep his family, he'd go to counseling. Period.

Not that I would have gone right out and gotten a divorce otherwise. I'm sad over how easily and quickly couples are driven to such a place. The truth is, I'm not sure what I would have done (besides go on a fast and get on my face and cry out to God in earnest to save my marriage). I'm glad we never got to that point, or even close. But I hope I wouldn't have resigned myself to merely coexisting with Dave under the same roof, detached from each other in a dead marriage. There are too many testimonies of the miraculous in this area to give up so soon.

Best-selling novelist Debbie Macomber is one such example. Her marriage had ended, and she and Wayne were going through the process of divorce. In the meantime she felt God was speaking to her to commit to praying for one hour a day for a whole year. She stuck to her commitment and prayed on her knees every day for 365 days. God honored her faithful obedience by restoring her marriage completely. Today Debbie and Wayne Macomber are a thriving testimony of the power of God to restore broken marriages.[4]

Of course, these are sensitive and complex issues for many couples. Friends have told me of marriage complications that leave my head spinning. My heart breaks, and all I can do is pray for them. One thing I pray is that they don't give up too easily and quickly and that they'll be willing to fight for their marriage and family. I include the two together because a broken marriage means a broken family. Remember, this book is about loving our children. How hard and long are we willing to work to give them a secure and happy home?

And Yet...

My daughter struggles with addiction. Her drug of choice? Breast milk. While I long to clear the space in bed between hubby's warm body and mine, I am still satisfying an eighteen-month-old's urge to suck...suck...suck.

I know she doesn't need it. It's just that life hasn't afforded me the opportunity to send her to "rehab" in a room of her own. Our family of four shares a bedroom in my mother-in-law's house.

We are presently moving into our fifth house in five years. We manage rental properties and own fixer-upper houses in four different towns: Campbelltown, Newmanstown, Elizabethtown, and Middletown—all of which my son Judah conveniently and affectionately refer to using his own made-up name, "Pig-n-town."

"Mommy, are we going to 'Pig-n-town' today?" Oh, to rest in the peace of an ever-smiling child who never knows in which house he is going to sleep on any given night.

When it comes to the proper care and feeding of children, I have broken all the "rules." I missed the supposed magical "six months old" marker for getting my babies to sleep through the night. I am not Baby Wise or Mommy Wise or At-All Wise, it seems. Anyone keeping one- and three-year-olds in cloth diapers while living an "Are we there yet, God?" life may need to have her head examined.

And yet...There is always, bright on my horizon, the great "and yet."

"Yet I will rejoice" (Hab. 3:18). I rejoice because, somehow, in God's great mercy, and despite the fact that I can't seem to make homemaking look like it does on the cover of *Family Circle*...a still-sucking toddler and her slightly-confused-about-his-home-address big brother shout "hallelujah" in the midst of the chaos. They are my teachers. They know nothing but to sing and dance and hug whoever enters their personal space.

I have learned to name and count my blessings—among them, my children's laughter. It's a sound that produces a joy I could so easily forfeit for a bitter bowl of self-pity. Even as I sit in "tonight's house" and watch a team of ants busily dismantling a moth on the filthy carpet beneath me, even as I stare at my belly, swollen with new life, I know that God holds my hopes and dreams in His hands, and that any house where He reigns supreme is "home."

—GRACE NISSLEY

Who Takes Priority?

You may have gotten the impression by now that I believe the husband comes first—before the kids, the dog, and the dishes. And you'd be right. But what exactly does this mean?

I once heard a Christian radio broadcast on the subject. The guest on the show was suggesting that we verbally assign numerical values to our spouses and children, and regularly remind everyone in the family where they fall in line. "Johnny, I want you to know that your father is a ten in my eyes, and you and Beatrice are nines. He came before you, after all."

What?

Thankfully the show hostess challenged the guest's warped philosophy by saying, "Do you believe a couple can be great lovers but lousy parents?" I applauded her insight and wrote to thank her.

We parents who believe in keeping the marriage bed sacred need to make sure we stay balanced. I cannot imagine stating my children's worth to me in comparison to their father's in terms of numbers. The fact is, I love them all equally but differently. I couldn't bear to live without any of them, and I strive to show it in the way I treat them. That is, Dave and I are red-hot lovers, but I am just as passionate about nurturing my kids. One cannot and should not outweigh the other.

And yet we need to somehow let our children know that they are not the center of the universe. Mom and Dad are in charge—and in love. Kids feel secure knowing *these two things*. They want to know that Mom and Dad will always be together. We need to reassure them of that from time to time. Have you noticed how your little three-year-old will come running over the instant you and hubby start a hugging session by the kitchen sink? She squeezes herself right into the circle of love, because that's where she feels the most secure. Listen: *our children want us to put the marriage first.*

One evening Dave and I were headed out the door for a date night. When one of the girls began to complain about us leaving, I got down at her eye level, held her, and said, "Sweetie, there are plenty of kids who *wish* their moms and dads would date each other." I never heard another complaint about date night. In fact, nowadays the girls beg Dave and I to go out in order to score their own movie night complete with Kraft mac-and-cheese. They don't mind our date nights because we are careful to keep family nights at home as sacred as the marriage bed, making our kids feel they are important and precious to us.

But I Don't Have a Babysitter!

I highly recommend that couples have a weekly date night, but one of the most common objections I encounter is,

"But I don't have a babysitter!" There are plenty of good solutions for safe babysitting. Ask friends to recommend someone. Church and homeschool co-ops are also great places to find a mature, responsible caregiver for your children. If nothing else, trade off babysitting with a trusted friend or another couple. If a mom wants to cultivate the marriage relationship, she'll find a way to do it— unless she simply doesn't trust anyone to babysit.

Some moms hyperventilate at the thought of leaving their children with someone else; often that includes their own husbands (I am not referring to dads with a history of child abuse). It seems to be a deeper issue than not trusting a babysitter, though. A fearful and nervous disposition, I've observed, often goes hand in hand with mothers who are afraid to leave their kids in someone else's care. Babysitters are just one item on a mile-long list of things they worry about. They rush their little darlings to the doctor at lip's first quiver, and they lie awake at night wondering if some creep is going to try to snatch their kids on the way home from school.

One mother told me she didn't want to go on a camping trip to the Smoky Mountains because she was sure it would end in her child being eaten by bears. I thought it was a good idea—not feeding the child to the bears, but showing him bears in the wild. Fear robs our lives of many joys.

One of the joys mother-fear can rob us of is adult relationships. Look, I know what it can be like to leave kids in the hands of their daddy. I understand the risks. They may eat Jolly Ranchers for dinner and be allowed to slosh around in ice puddles wearing only T-shirts. A hailstorm of toys and dishes may blow through the house in your absence. The kids may stay up too late watching *Gladiator.* Their teeth may go un-brushed and their bottoms un-wiped. After the first time Dave gave Anna and Sarah a bath, I asked him, "Did you scrub their bottoms?"

"No, I didn't *scrub their bottoms,*" he said. "I let 'em soak." I nearly fainted. But they survived.

A God-Centered Home

The issue here is not whether we are going to have a child-centered home or a parent-centered home; what we want is a God-centered home. Keeping God at the center of your home means you trust Him with your children. You can leave your kids in the palm of God's hand while you tend to other important relationships. I can't emphasize it enough.

Too many mothers, in the name of wanting their kids to feel secure, take away from their kids the very thing they need to feel most secure—a loving, stable relationship between Mom and Dad. Not wanting to compromise their children's well-being, they stay close to home, never dating Dad for fear that something will go wrong in their absence. The fact is, sooner or later, much will go wrong in their controlling presence.

The need to be in control is directly associated with fear. The mom who can't get through a bucket of popcorn at the movies without worrying that her house has burned down in the hands of a qualified babysitter is a control freak racked with fear. That also goes for the mom who slathers her children's hands with Purell every thirty seconds and can't leave a child in the church nursery.

Now I'm preaching to myself! The thought of possibly allowing my daughters to be in the same room with a snotty-nosed, feverish kid makes my skin crawl. I am my children's valiant guardian against germs and all things harmful. But I have to continually remind myself that ultimately my kids and their safety and health lie not in my hands but in God's.

We would do well to rest and allow the peace of God to govern our thoughts toward the care of our children. God is well able to protect our kids—even in our absence. Sometimes I think He is *better* able then!

 Refrigerator Magnet: A God-centered home is a secure environment in which my husband is honored and my children are nurtured.

 Heart Exam: In what area(s) do I need to fully relinquish control and place my family in God's trustworthy hands?

Chapter 9

THE OTHER "S" WORD

I TOLD A FRIEND that I was writing a couple chapters on discipline and was going to bravely touch on spanking. "Do you have to use the word *spank*?" she wondered.

I gave it some thought and said, "I suppose I could try 'the physical application of correction to the derriere.'"

I understood my friend's fear of what might become of me if I write about sp—sp—spanking. People get in trouble for that sort of thing. The last thing I want to do is create certain images in people's minds by admitting I believe there's still a time and place for corporal punishment. I wonder if readers will picture me living in a commune, sharing Dave with seven other wives, beating my kids into submission on a daily basis.

May I ask you a favor? If the idea of spanking makes you roll your eyes or causes your stomach to turn, can you, for a moment, entertain the following possibilities?

1. I love and seek to nurture my children as much as you do yours.

2. I am not "just another fundamentalist" raising hate-filled, violence-loving citizens.

3. I rarely spank.

4. My kids are glad I spank. (Ask them.)

5. My kids wish more parents would spank. (They tell me that.)

6. I got spanked, and I'm eternally grateful.

7. I don't believe all parents should spank.

In my introduction I said this book is not another how-to on being a great mother. I meant that. It is rather about fully embracing motherhood and loving your kids. Plenty of moms don't have "warm fuzzies" in regard to their children. I've had mothers tell me they can't wait until their kids are gone. One mom said she surfed the Internet to try to find a place to send her troublesome little girl away. Another confessed to feeling hatred toward her little boy.

I well understand what drives parents to those sentiments. I also believe much of our feelings of ill will toward our kids have to do with the issue of discipline. So I cannot write a book about falling in love with our children unless I address the topic in this and the following chapter.

I'm asking you to stop and pray for a minute if need be. Ask God to give you an open mind and heart to hear what I'm about to say—or at least ask Him to help you refrain from murdering the author of this book. You may not agree on all points in this section. Feel free to spit out what you might consider "bones" and eat what tender pieces of "meat" you may find in this chapter.

I don't pretend to be the authority on "authority." And I'm aware there are special needs kids to whom this chapter will not apply. But for the rest, before deciding I'm completely old-fashioned and out of touch, or worse, a proponent of child abuse, *if you feel that one more temper tantrum or screaming fit from your child is going to send you over the edge, or if you are tired of dealing with a child who stubbornly refuses to budge—keep reading.*

Discipline and Punishment— Understanding the Difference

The word *discipline* is taboo for many postmodern parents. Like the word *authority*, it may connote a stern taskmaster carrying a switch. A kid-beater might come to mind. For many, it carries the idea of punishment—maybe even cruel punishment—depending on your upbringing. My friend Georgia was "disciplined" by being forced to stand against a wall all night balancing a quarter on her nose. When she nodded off and the quarter slipped to the floor one too many times, she was forced, as a kid, to drink strong, black coffee into the wee hours of the morning in order to stay awake. That, my friend, is not discipline.

My friend "Rosemary's" mom used to fly off the handle and switch up and down Rosemary's bare legs, matching each angry word with a strike: "If-I-ever-catch-you-doing-that-a-gain-I'm-going-to-beat-your-tail-off." Then she'd throw the switch down and leave the room. Rosemary ran outside during one such episode and screamed, "Help! Call the police!" Her mother never switched her again. That is not discipline either. It's punishment.

Punishment is, well, punitive.

> Punish: From Latin *punire*—to inflict [cause pain] for (an offense)[1]

Contrast that with the meaning of the word *discipline*:

> Discipline: From Latin *disciplina*—training that corrects, molds, or perfects the mental faculties or moral character[2]

Do those two definitions look at all alike to you? Let's get first things first: *discipline is not punitive*. It is not something you do *to* a child, but rather it's something you do *for* a child. It is what a good teacher uses if she wants her student to learn and grow. Moms, in a sense, are teachers raising blood-related or adopted students. If we love them, we'll discipline them. Loving discipline has relatively little to do with pain (though it may involve physical pain) and everything to do with training and nurturing.

Discipline comes in many forms, and I believe it's important to identify which unique methods of discipline each child will respond to best. The possibilities are endless, and it takes creativity and gathering ideas from fellow moms or respected resources on the subject.

Why Discipline?

Before I get into what discipline looks like, let's make sure we understand why it's important. If you don't know why discipline is important, just go to the mall and hang out on a bench in front of a toy store for a while. Inevitably you'll see demonstrated in front of you why children need discipline. You may see a young mom dragging her three-year-old out of the store, trying to pry a Nerf blaster from his grasp before the security alarm goes off. He'll scream and throw himself on the floor and maybe kick Mom in the shin.

But she's bigger and stronger and patient a little longer, so she'll pick him up, carry him out, sit next to you on that bench, and wrestle little boss down against his will, promising him an ice cream if he'll stop crying. Eventually he'll stop, and they'll walk down to Baskin Robbins. When you hear him scream again, you'll know they're out of the bubble gum flavor. If you were to follow this pair a few years into the future, at worst this mom may eventually check out emotionally and leave the kid to do whatever he wants in his preteen years, likely with disastrous consequences. At best you may watch the boy carry his own kid out of a toy store and into an I Scream shop because, in all fairness, that's how Mom did it.

That *is* how moms do it, right? Even Super Nanny does it that way! Speak in a submissive tone and constrict him until he gets himself under control, no matter how many hours or days or weeks or months it takes. Try not to think about how hard this is going to be ten years down the road. Oh, yes, there will still be tantrums—just of a different kind. "Discipline your children while there is hope. Otherwise you will ruin their lives" (Prov. 19:18, NLT).

Aren't Tantrums a Normal Part of Childhood?

I have a confession to make. Before I do, promise not to hate me. I completely understand your desire to hate me once I say what I'm going to say, but let's make a deal: if after I say this you don't hate me, I'll try and help you get to the place where you can make a similar confession. And that is this: *none of my four children have ever thrown a single temper tantrum.*

For that matter, neither did I nor my siblings, nor did many of my friends and their children. (Tell me when the tomatoes are gone and I can come out from hiding.)

I know you are less fond of me for saying that, but hear me out: I understand the general consensus—even among Christian parenting experts—is that daily tantrums are a normal part of childhood. I fully respect that. Also, I am not suggesting the reason we had no tantrums in our household is solely due to spanking. What I *am* saying and want you to realize is that no-tantrum families *are possible.*

We humans have been around for hundreds of years and will continue to exist. Amish children, for example, are generally regarded as well-mannered, happy, and highly nurtured kids in a society where spankings are administered as the main form of discipline, not that the same kind of discipline necessarily needs to be the case with us. What I am saying is that if those parents don't accept thrashing fits in the candy aisle of the grocery store as a norm for the average child's behavior, why should we?

While I'm saying this, I also want to be careful *not to inflict guilt or feelings of failure on mothers who deal with temper tantrums.* Believe me, when I see a mom wrestling with a screaming child, I know she is doing her very best as a mother. I'm not sitting there judging her child's "lack of discipline." I'm taking into consideration that there may be a host of factors unknown to me: that child may be sick, exhausted, or autistic—the possibilities are endless (including the fact that spanking is illegal in much of an increasingly secularized Europe, so moms from certain cultures may not even consider it). When I see a mother struggling with a child throwing a tantrum, I admire her for not giving up the fight! So *I give you my pledge to relate to you with the same tenderness and understanding I need as a fellow mom.*

I Am Nothing Special, and Neither Are My Kids!

I care deeply about moms and want them to enjoy the peace that comes with having well-behaved kids. I didn't say "perfect" children. (If you have those, *I'm* throwing tomatoes!)

I know what you may be thinking:

- "Faith, you have all girls. Girls are sugar and spice."

- "Your girls are nice. They are sweet and gentle, just like their ~~mom~~ dad."

- "You got lucky enough to give birth to four angels." (No one is ever that lucky!)

- "You have a lot of support, with a very involved husband and all. Of course your kids are well-behaved." (Some of the brattiest kids I know have two very involved and in-love parents. By the same token, some of the most well-behaved kids I know are being raised by single moms.)

• "You have the energy to discipline." (Most of my discipline does not involve the use of any gross motor skills, especially now that my kids are getting older.)

The truth is, my children were born just like yours—as human beings. They are, like each of us, capable of the worst kind of behavior. And yet, *after fifteen years of parenting, not one of my kids has ever screamed in order to get her way.* How did Dave and I do that? How did the "accidental parents" who hardly know what they're doing most of the time do that?

For starters, *we* didn't *do that.* Much of the time I'm on my face begging God to help me figure this out. We pray a lot, and God has helped us. If our kids are at all great, it is because we seek a great God.

Secondly, we had good role models. And this is where I can only hope you come away with a different perspective on spanking and see that I am not, in fact, a barbaric parent or discipline snob. I'm simply using what I learned growing up (which was based on Scripture) along with the wisdom of other moms and a few good books thrown in.

When I Was Growing Up

I was born into a pastor's home with more rules than the Code of Hammurabi: Don't use too many sheets of toilet paper. Scrape the peanut butter jar clean. Brush your teeth—brush them all day long. No dating until you're thirty. No prancing around in painted-on jeans or short shorts. No eating sweets or refined foods or you'll die of cancer. No sleeping in or staying up late. No curfew. (When you can't go out in the first place, there's no need for a curfew.) No secular music. No movies. No TV. No dancing. No, no, no, no, no!

Now, with rules like those, I was supposed to rebel, right? I should have run away, pierced my cheek with a dog bone, and tattooed my tongue. Or at best, I should have turned out to be one of those moms who's afraid her children might rebel if she dares assume authority: "Sweetie, I'd prefer you don't jump off the balcony. You could get hurt. Make the right choice. That's one. Two. Three...."

But I did none of the above, even though my parents spanked me. I figured that was what good parents did. Dad carved a wooden paddle and started applying it to my behind as soon as I could say, "No, I won't!" His spankings were carefully thought out. Far from flying off the handle and beating me silly, he'd calmly send me to my bedroom to wait for him. (One time I locked the door and put on every pair of underwear I owned to pad my buns before Dad arrived.)

Dad would come in with the paddle, sit beside me on the bed, hold me close, and gently ask if I understood why I was being disciplined. I always said yes and meant it. *I don't recall ever feeling like I didn't deserve a spanking.* He'd ask me to quote Proverbs 22:15: "Foolishness is bound in the heart of a child; but the rod of correction shall drive it far from him" (KJV). Then he'd tell me how many licks I was going to get before laying me across his lap and delivering them. There were usually between three and five whacks—depending on the offense, on how much I resisted, and on the tears.

The type of tears I cried was important. Dad knew the difference between angry "ouch!" tears and repentant tears. He could tell which were tears of *regret* (sadness that I got caught) and which were tears of *remorse* (real sorrow for wrongdoing). He knew the difference, and so did I. There was a certain sound in my cry that Dad was looking for: a brokenness, not of a broken spirit but of a broken will.

Dad's spankings left me with blushing "cheeks" and a tender heart—never a single bruise or welt. They always, without exception, concluded with him holding me on his lap for a while, tight against his chest and telling me how much he loved me. I never doubted it and always felt a deep sense of relief that, though it was painful, my "sin" had been found out and accounted for. There was a cleansing that took place in my soul that I recognized, even as a small child. "By the wounds of the rod evil is taken away, and blows make clean the deepest parts of the body" (Prov. 20:30, BBE).

Because discipline was practiced *in the medium of love and nurturing,* not only did I not rebel, but also I grew up to discipline my children in similar manner (though not nearly as often; this chapter is purposed to *explore the topic of spanking without necessarily presenting it as the main means of discipline*). It was the same with many of my friends. We understand the truth behind what author Josh McDowell said: "Rules without relationship equal rebellion."[3] Or, I could say, "One part spanking without four parts affection equals even worse behavior!" It is as

Ephesians 6:4 says, "Fathers, do no exasperate your children; instead, bring them up in the training and instruction of the Lord."

The spankings tapered off as I grew out of early childhood. It was the same for John and Grace, my younger siblings. Paul, the baby of the family, hardly ever got spanked, if at all. Parents soften with age, like piecrust, and besides, Paul had a gentle disposition and compliant nature. I'd wonder if he was adopted were it not for his sheer genius so obviously like his oldest sibling's.

I still remember my last "spanking." I don't remember the offense, but I recall Dad standing there with the paddle, getting ready to whack my young-lady behind. I stood there, all five-foot-something of me, and just looked at him. We'd become the best of friends. He couldn't do it; I was too old. We both burst out laughing, and I knew it was over for good. Restrictions and other methods of discipline replaced spankings from then on.

I never questioned whether I should be getting spanked. It didn't occur to me to compare spanking to abuse or being "hit." That idea never entered the radar. As much as I hated being spanked, *I knew with all of my heart that it was right* and that it was making me an easier child to live with—and a better human being, for that matter.

Spanking in My House

So when I had my own daughter, I naturally used spanking as one of our means of discipline. Dave was in agreement; he was also raised in a "spanking home." We began by swatting Anna's behind when she was old enough to toddle into perceivable trouble. We did this in the following circumstances:

- For *repeat offenses* (it's important to simply say no the first time; some humans are quicker than others at getting a clue). Anna would eye some forbidden object—say, her sister's eyeball. She'd look our way to see what we'd do if she tried once again to remove it. As her little claws moved toward the baby's face, one of us would lightly smack the back of her fat hand (if a diaper prevented her from feeling a swat on her bottom). We did this hard enough to leave a little sting; then we'd firmly say, "No!" She got the message.

  (Note and disclaimer: There are varying views on whether one should "spank" a child's hand or spank using the parent's hand versus a paddle or other object. I'd much rather point you to the trusted experts listed in the resources section at the back of this book than pontificate on how to spank. I am simply sharing my story with you to make a case for appropriate biblical discipline.)

- *When there was no better alternative.* In the previous example, we would have naturally sought first to remove the temptation—place the eyeball-containing baby out of harm's way or else place the tempted two-year-old in temporary confinement. But there are times neither of those is possible: the baby is in a stationary swing, for example, or the leash to tie up the older sibling has gone missing (I'm kidding!).

I could have responded by constantly pulling my kids away from mischief (in cases where there was no play yard available, for example, to make my job easier) and wearied myself in the process. There are a lot of tired moms walking around this planet. I hope to do what little I can to change that.

Some mothers take spanking to an extreme and, instead of removing the marble from the floor, slap the baby's hand every time she tries to pick it up. I trust you have more brains than that. Do yourself a favor and baby-proof your home. The day will come when you can light that yummy candle and put out those porcelain figurines again.

Would I Spank?

Whenever I misbehaved in public, my dad would give me The Look. Nothing rivaled its wide-eyed intensity. Along with The Look, a number of fingers were raised to indicate the level of discipline I'd receive when I got home. One finger meant one swat was imminent—chastisement "lite." Two swats was industry standard. Three swats was maximum sentence, administered for particularly grievous offences, such as disrespecting Mom. Dad didn't like that. Talking back, disobeying, a "bad attitude," strife, and whining were the other cardinal sins of my early childhood.

Dad was the chief administrator of discipline in the house. We kids would beg Mom to spank us. "Please don't wait for Dad to get home! Spank us now and get it over with," we'd cry. Not only would it hang over our heads, but there was also the little matter that Dad spanked a lot harder than Mom.

If I did something wrong and didn't get spanked for it, it bothered me. Sometimes I'd go to my parents and confess so I could get the spanking over with and the transgression off my mind. They always gave me a hug, and we'd pray together afterward. This showed me that all was forgiven on their part and reinforced to me that the pain they inflicted was out of love, not anger. And if I was being particularly stubborn, having to pray aloud usually broke that, because my parents didn't let me get away with a mumbled half-hearted prayer. I had to mean it.

Today I'm a college student living at home, and I have a great relationship with my parents. Their consistency in discipline is one of the greatest gifts they gave me. Among the things I learned while laid across my parents' laps is utmost respect for every human and the need to take responsibility for my actions.

Someone asked me if I will spank my kids when I have them. Does the sun rise in the east? Do bears sleep in the woods? Perhaps the sun rising in the east is based on my frame of reference. Perhaps bears sleep in the woods because that is where they grew up. But I am without doubt going to spank my kids.

—ANDREW PEARSON

Consistency Pays

I remember the time a young family visited us and spent the night in our master bedroom. Dave and I were down the hall and heard the dad spank their child in an effort to get him to stop whining and go to sleep. It worked like magic. The next morning at breakfast the subject came up. "We've found the more you consistently spank, the less you have to," the father told us. Though I was a spanker myself, I was also a new parent. I thought what he said was the dumbest thing I'd ever heard. It was like saying, "The more you jump up and down, the less you have to."

But his words proved amazingly true! Since Dave and I were consistent to discipline our kids in those first few years, spankings are rare—*rare*—in our house nowadays. (It may not sound like it because of the length I'm going to in discussing it here. Trust me, if you spank enough in the beginning, you hardly ever have to do it later on.) We are enjoying the fruits of our paddling labor and often receive compliments on the girls' behavior.

A word of wisdom: This will take extreme patience and sacrifice. It is not always convenient to discipline using *any method.* Be prepared to eat a lot of cold meals as you're training your son to stay in his booster seat or to quit slinging peas across the room. It's so much easier to take the easy way out by feeding him Goldfish or letting him eat on the floor with the dog. But it will be well worth it in the long run.

Cold dinners at home now may mean peaceful dinners out later on. This is the season of planting. Spanking is one of our God-given instruments, if used wisely, for sowing seeds of righteousness. There is a harvest of good behavior coming! "No discipline seems pleasant at the time, but painful. Later on, however, it produces a harvest of righteousness and peace for those who have been trained by it" (Heb. 12:11).

What Merits a Spanking?

Of course we try to use other methods of discipline as a primary resort. I'll get to that. But first, let me explain what has merited a spanking in the Bogdan household:

- **Disregard for safety.** If a swift, hard-felt swat on buns will keep my child from drowning, being hit by a car, or crushed under a towering bookshelf, I'm going to spank. Plain and simple.

- **Violence.** This is any willful, physical harming of a human being. Biting, kicking, or hitting means an automatic spanking. Some may ask, "But isn't that hypocritical? Aren't you using violence to punish violence?" It's no more hypocritical than a police officer using handcuffs to shackle the hands that tied up a hostage. The answer is, "No, I'm using spanking to correct violence." Children understand this difference better than many adults do.

- **Sassiness or blatant disrespect.** This is rare in our household since my girls have learned that behind every burning bottom may be a tongue that has chosen to "dis" the mother or father.

- **Defiance.** A "no, I won't" attitude warrants an immediate trip to the bathroom to await one's just reward on the throne of doom.

(Again, this is rare, because proper spanking works.)

• **Whining.** This is where I see parents missing out on the opportunity for *any kind* of discipline the most. Parents' tolerance level for whining is much too high. Kids should know that no means no. One mother told her child, "I don't speak 'Whinese.'" Personally, I ask my kids to do something *once* with my words and the *second* time (not the thirtieth time) with the paddle. (Again, as they get older, I find that other means of discipline are just as effective. Stay tuned for that in the next chapter.)

How You Spank Makes All the Difference

When a mother on the brink of insanity with an out-of-control child is seeking my advice, I sometimes get around to asking, "Do you spank?" Often she'll say, "Yes, but it doesn't work." Upon further questioning, I discover she employs the all-too-common "spanking lite" method. That is, she uses the equivalent of a Popsicle stick to deliver a tap on the child's Pull-up. He in turn runs away giggling at the fact that he's fooled his mother into believing spankings don't work. Of course *those* kinds don't work. "Don't fail to discipline your children. They won't die if you spank them. Physical discipline may well save them from death" (Prov. 23:13–14, NLT).

Spankings kind of need to hurt in order for a change in behavior to occur. If they don't leave the child with a willingness to say, through real tears, "I'm sorry, Mommy," you may be spanking your child, but you're not disciplining him.

However, we should never expect to hear those words from our children if we can't say them ourselves. To the degree we parents can look our kids in the eyes and humbly own our stuff when we're wrong, getting on the floor and kissing their feet if need be, we can expect them to receive correction from us. This is more and more important the older they get.

Abuse

Let me be clear: I'm not talking about abuse—that is, spanking your child on any part of his body other than that padded place God conveniently created to receive instruction (or the back of the hand, when appropriate, as in the earlier example). Furthermore, discipline does not involve leaving bruises or welts on children. And it shouldn't be done in public; I'm not interested in humiliating my child. If a behavior merits a spanking and I'm in the store or in church, for example, I might deliver a tiny pinch on the underside of my daughter's thigh and she gets the message instantly. It's important for discipline to occur immediately, especially with smaller children, so they make the connection with the misbehavior.

Most importantly, spanking should never involve anger. I have often found it necessary to send one of my kids to her room to wait while I cool down and prepare my heart to discipline properly. If Dave is at home when one of the girls needs immediate hind-end attention, I often hand him the paddle and walk away. His forbearance allows him to sit with a child for a while and talk tenderly about what she did before he finally spanks her. I'm hoping to become that kind of patient person, but it's taking so long!

When Spanking Doesn't Work

Spankings may cease to work on some children, giving more reason to seek alternative methods of discipline. When Anna was very small, we eventually realized she'd become "immune" to spankings. We'd warn her not to venture into forbidden territory, and she'd look at us as if to say, "Watch me." She'd commit the offense, and one of us would swat her hand enough to leave a sting, and she'd stare back with an expression that clearly read, "That was cool! Do it again!"

It's not that she was a strong-willed child (her otherwise gentle disposition told us so); she simply had inherited her father's high pain threshold and extreme curiosity about the elements of the physical world around her. Her policy was that toddling into some restricted zone was always worth the risk of a little pain. Perhaps we could have been tougher, but we didn't have to wonder for long. Anna quickly outgrew this behavior, to our great relief.

Sarah, on the other hand, was super sensitive. Often we didn't even have to go through with the spanking. All it took was to give her "the look." Her lips would tremble, and she'd break into sobs, as if to say "I'll never do it again!" even if she hadn't done it yet. But that was also only while Sarah was very small.

It has been our experience that children go through different stages in regard to how they respond to spanking. As Sarah got older, her need for discipline did not lessen, but she stopped responding to spankings altogether. I realized that if I spanked her for every wrongdoing, she'd have no backside left. We had to discover what methods of training worked for her.

Anna's need for any kind of discipline decreased significantly as she got older. She and Rebecca inherited Dave's easy-going nature; Sarah and Ruthie did not. It was a woman named Laurel Thatcher Ulrich who wrote a book called *Well-Behaved Women Seldom Make History.*[4] If that's true, Sarah and Ruthie are going to be world-famous tomorrow, along with their mother.

 Refrigerator Magnet: It is better to raise the paddle than to raise your voice.

 Heart Exam: In what way(s) do I tend to punish my children while not actually disciplining them?

Chapter 10

TAILOR-MADE DISCIPLINE

I F THE PREVIOUS chapter was bothersome, let's just move on. If you feel spanking isn't right for you, explore other options with me in the next few pages.

As I mentioned, spankings stopped working for Sarah early on. Restrictions don't always work either. I can hide her book and threaten to banish her from the library for the rest of her life, and she will still take four hours to complete a thirty-minute task, and that half-heartedly. I have had to figure out what *does* work.

For Sarah, it's a tangible, immediate reward. The one thing she will do anything for—even obey—is sugar. She inherited my love for all things sweet. So the other day I pointed out a fresh baked pie cooling on the stove and said, "Sarah, to the degree that you quickly and thoroughly clean this kitchen, you will enjoy a generous slice of pie for dessert tonight." I came back a half hour later and almost fainted; the countertops looked clean enough to lick. Sarah doesn't need Ritalin—she needs *pie.*

"How is that discipline?" you ask. Experience has taught Sarah that if she does not obey, she shall have no pie. There were no exceptions in the past; neither will there be today. Through the use of rewards she is being instructed— disciplined—in the area of obedience. Of course that method is not *all* we use with Sarah, or her teeth would have rotted and fallen out long ago. I confess I struggle to come up with ways to effectively discipline her—including other types of rewards—almost on a daily basis. I am simply sharing with you what I have learned so far.

I try to use rewards as much as, if not more than, negative reinforcement. Discipline doesn't have to be all unpleasant. For instance, before I take the girls into a gift shop or to lunch at someone's house, I'll sometimes say, "We're playing the Compliment Game!" That means whoever gets complimented on good manners receives a prize. The girls love this. Inevitably a stranger will say something like, "My, what well-behaved kids you have!" At that point the girls will beam at me and one another as if to say, "*Yesssss!* We're gettin' Kit Kats, baby!" I simply thank the person and pretend my girls are always that angelic. But the habit of good manners is sticking as they outgrow their need for such compliments and rewards.

Different Strokes for Different Daughters

As with siblings in all families, Anna's behavioral issues are different from Sarah's. I am learning not to mistake her need for one-on-one attention with a need for discipline. (This can also be true with Sarah; it takes divine wisdom to know what's going on in each situation.) Too many times I've slapped a restriction or warning on Anna, only to see her behavior worsen. (For her, bad behavior usually means rolling the eyes and distancing herself from me.)

I'm learning that more often than not her errant attitude is the result of a mother who is too busy. All it takes is removing my authoritarian hat and giving her a foot massage, talking about girly stuff like which guys I'd let her date, and—voilà! She's a new girl with a tender heart *and* tender feet. (If you haven't already, I highly recommend familiarizing yourself with *The 5 Love Languages*.[1] This has been a tremendous help in knowing how to relate to individual family members. If you have read Dr. Gary Chapman's books, you might have guessed already that one of Sarah's love languages is "receiving gifts," especially if they're sweet! Dave prefers "quality time," and Anna responds well to "physical touch.")

Rebecca and Ruthie are Anna and Sarah all over again, respectively. And I am in trouble, because at age forty-one I'm softening on my "baby." I may need to read this and the previous chapter a few times for myself. Ruthie is cute and has some Facebook-worthy things to say, but she still needs discipline. The paddle has not been put away for good.

Consequences

Before we get into consequences, I'll touch on the "1-2-3 Magic" method in case you're wondering if counting 1-2-3 as you give your children a chance to obey is a good idea. I can't verify that it's true, but I can certainly imagine the following scenario happening: I once heard a story on the radio of a little boy going after his ball in the road. His mother called him back and he didn't budge, so she started counting, "One..." The child knew he had until three to obey and sadly was hit by a car that appeared out of nowhere while he was waiting to hear that magic number. (One wonders why the mother didn't simply snatch the child away from danger and skip the counting.) I believe we should teach our children immediate—not delayed—obedience. When I sense God is telling me to do something, I don't hear Him saying, "You have until three."

What about the "Time Out" chair? It works well; I send myself there on a daily basis! Seriously, I've used it on occasion and particularly in instances when I felt a spanking wasn't warranted. Of course, the idea presupposes that the child will actually sit and stay there. If not, that's when spanking comes in handy.

Now that my kids are getting older, Dave and I are moving toward a "punishment fits the crime" philosophy. This is very effective. For example: if one of our daughters is caught being deceptive, she may be asked to find a Bible verse on lying and write it a number of times (killing two birds with one stone; she now has another memory verse under her belt). She may have to write an essay on bullying if she continues to call her sister names.

We have a collection container on top of the fridge where light switch abusers can "donate" to our electricity fund. Or if the child is young and penniless, a different way to address wasting electricity is to remove her bedroom light bulb for a time whenever she leaves the light on (and no, she may *not* roast mini marshmallows with a candle in her bed!).

In our house discipline is often a simple "abuse it, lose it" matter. If Baby Girl texts while driving after her sixteenth birthday next year, guess who gets to keep her phone or keys for a while. It may sound tough, but dealing with a tragic accident would be a lot tougher. Someone makes a smoothie and doesn't rinse the blender out and leaves banana peels on the countertop for Mom the maid to clean up? No smoothie the next day. Someone leaves the cream cheese out? Guess who's having a plain bagel tomorrow. They fight over the last brownie? Mom takes it (and eats it). She doesn't stand there and wear herself out playing judge over whom it rightfully belongs to (unless I can quickly and easily determine that; I do try to be reasonable).

I practice "Creative Correction" *à la* Lisa Whelchel, who wrote a book by that name.[2] If the girls are bickering with one another, I make them sit side by side on the couch together, holding hands, whispering whatever "sweet nothing" I prescribe: "I'll love you forever, and I'm glad you're my sister." Maybe this sounds like cruel and unusual punishment (and you know your own kids), but do you know what? Without fail, after a few minutes my girls end up laughing and are back to being friends. They know our biggest household rule is that *we get along.*

They haven't exactly told me this to my face, but I know my children appreciate this uncomplicated, common-sense method of discipline. If one girl breaks another's toy or loses a belonging, she simply replaces it or gives up her matching set. If she destroys someone's Littlest Pet Shop village, she rebuilds it. If we're visiting someone's home and one of my kids spills her drink, she cleans it up and apologizes to the host.

Apologies are important—even if it was an accident. You'd be surprised (no, you wouldn't) how often a child will do something like step on a toe and not see the need to apologize on the grounds of it being an accident. One would think she'd understand that if I accidentally stepped on her pet chicken I'd still need to say, "I'm sorry." I have actually had to explain that.

Just Write the Ticket Already!

Back to sensible consequences. Someone once said that discipline should be like a police officer calmly writing a ticket. That ticket will speak louder to the driver than a freak-show tongue-lashing. ("Dontchoo *ever* let me catch you speeding again, young lady, or I'll tell your daddy and slam your bootay in the can!") I try to keep that in mind and let consequences speak instead of the words that would just as soon fly out of my mouth.

If Anna wants to go bowling with the youth group but doesn't have her homework done, she stays home. She's out of clean laundry because she failed to wash her clothes? She'll have to wear whatever she can find. Ruthie escapes the car empty-handed after being asked to help bring in the groceries? She gets to clean out the entire car. Sarah is caught reading during her live cyber school class? I confiscate her book. Rebecca's playing Mario before her homework is done? I take her laptop for the rest of the day. Someone complains about what we're watching for a family night movie? No problem! She doesn't have to watch it. She goes to bed.

One time Dave and I wrote the girls a hefty "ticket" because they weren't ready to leave the house on time. We were going, as a family, to our Bible study at church. The girls always look forward to this because doughnuts are served during group discussion. (Have I mentioned how spiritual my daughters are?) I gave them plenty of warning, calling to them up the stairs where they were dawdling, and said, "We are driving out of here in exactly five minutes! Whoever is not in the car will stay home."

Five minutes later Dave and I got in the car with one daughter and drove off. Not one of them has ever since made us wait. Of course, they were old enough to stay home alone.

My friend Deborah understands that consequences are among the world's best teachers. The other day she was shopping in Kohl's and used one of the scanner devices (located throughout the store for customer use) to check the availability of an item online. Her five-year-old son, Regis, found the keypad buttons irresistible. Deborah warned him, "Do not touch those buttons!" But what child does not push buttons?

Regis inadvertently summoned a sales clerk for help. I suppose some parents, at worst, would have scuttled away and reprimanded their child behind the rack of scarves. At best, one might sheepishly apologize to the inconvenienced associate. But Deborah is wise to discipline; Regis had to explain to the clerk, from between his mother's legs, that he'd pushed the call button and that he was sorry. You can be sure that Regis will treat scanners and mothers who use them with a lot more respect from now on.

Does this put the word *discipline* in a new light? Our voice and blood pressure don't have to be raised through the roof. Good discipline means we are emotionally on top of training our kids in excellent character and behavior. We care enough to patiently turn out responsible and positive contributors to society. And we are doing a favor for our kids' future spouses, bosses, and the children they themselves will parent someday. Hey, I'm investing in pleasant grandkids! As Proverbs 29:17 tells us,

"Discipline your children, and they will give you peace of mind and will make your heart glad" (NLT).

The Heart-to-Heart Talk

If you are realizing the need to begin properly disciplining your child, you may want to sit down with him and have a little heart-to-heart that goes something like this (consider taking him to McDonald's and make it official, a landmark in his life):

"Sweetheart, I've been getting something backward for a while, and I need to switch it around. I've been letting you be the boss of this home and family. But actually, I am the one in charge (or 'Daddy and I' if you are married). It hasn't been working too well, me being your servant, has it, sweetie? I think we're both tired of our yelling and crying, and we need peace and happiness in our house. Since I am older and have a lot more experience in life, and since I am your mother, I need to be the boss."

At this point he should break down in tears of relief and thank you with a big hug. Well, maybe not. But rest assured, he knows the truth. Don't be moved by any cover-up. No buying him a sundae if he whines!

"Now, honey, as your mother I am going to start to do something that all good mothers do and that I should have done long ago. I'm going to discipline you." Explain the meaning of discipline as I did in the previous chapter. If you are going to include spanking, let him know what to expect. That is *very* important. To spank a child without proper communication at the age of understanding is abusive.

I've said something like this to my daughter before: "I'm

going to spank you because if I don't, you're going to turn out to be a real brat, and people don't enjoy being around brats. Then you're going to become a grown-up brat, and, believe me, I know a lot of grown-up brats. They have a hard time making and keeping friends, and they get fired from their jobs a lot, because they still have the idea that they are the boss of everyone, and they want to have their way all the time. But you are not going to be like that. You are my angel. I love you too much to let that happen."

You will want to continue this conversation for a while as you go through the process of retraining your child. If you're consistent, I promise you a new kid in no time. (Dr. Kevin Leman promises one by Friday.[3]) Before you get started, I'd like to let you in on my latest disciplining incident, to show you once more what it looks like and give you hope that this actually will work and bring peace to your home.

Discipline Works!

Last night we were on the couch watching a movie, all six of us. Ruthie demanded that Rebecca move so she could sit in Rebecca's place beside me. Ruthie had been sitting in that spot for a while and I thought Rebecca should have a turn. Besides, Ruthie could sit on the other side and they could both be next to me.

But Ruthie insisted on sitting to my right, where Rebecca had already staked her reasonable claim. Ruthie began to whine. I looked her in the eyes and gave a stern warning: "If you speak of this one more time, you're going to your room and missing the movie."

She quieted down and I thought we were OK. A

minute later she began to whimper. I firmly said, "Go. Now." She left the living room, crying, and went upstairs to bed. A few minutes later Rebecca asked if she could go kiss her sister good night. (This was, sadly, a punishment for Rebecca, whose soul is conjoined to her sister's like a Siamese twin. They are such inseparable friends I call to them as a unit: "Rebukie! Come and eat!")

I allowed her to do so, which set off another round of tears from Ruthie, who sent Rebecca back downstairs to call on me. I paused the movie for my patient family and went to Ruthie's bedside, where I found her red-eyed and attempting to bargain her way back downstairs to sit *any-where* on the couch.

Calmly I said, "I have to keep my word, Ruthie. If I let you come back downstairs, I'm a liar. Now the next time you call me up here, I'm coming with the paddle." And because I've always been consistent with the paddle (meaning, when I say I'm going to use it, I use it), she hushed. I tucked her in, closed the door, and we watched our movie in peace. I didn't have to spank. That's what my friend meant when he said, "The more you do it, the less you have to."

I should note that after the movie, when I went to tuck Rebecca in her bunk above Ruthie, I saw that Ruthie was still awake. She reached out for a hug and kiss, and we enjoyed a warm and tender few minutes of cuddling. There was no bitterness on her part or anger on mine. She hadn't hot-lined me and I hadn't screamed words of regret. *We were both experiencing the bliss of proper discipline.*

In conclusion, let me say again that I have not arrived at perfection in this area. Discipline is still *the biggest challenge* for me as a mother. I am always tweaking my methods and trying to figure out what works for each of my girls. I know it's the same for you. The good thing is, when we're feeling clueless as to how to get our kids to obey, we can fall to our knees and ask God for practical wisdom. He made each one of our children; "Father" knows best what will work for them! Remember James 1:5: "If you need wisdom, ask our generous God, and he will give it to you. He will not rebuke you for asking" (NLT).

 Refrigerator Magnet: I am the boss around here.

 Heart Exam: Am I willing to do the hard work of discipline, keeping my sights on the reward of enjoying my child for a lifetime?

Chapter 11

FAMILY DEVOTIONS—
ELIMINATING THE
YAWN FACTOR

I N CHAPTER 5 I said that the chief enterprise of a Christian mom is making God-lovers out of those entrusted to her care. This takes time, skill, prayer, wisdom—and "family devotions."

> Devotions: Religious observance or worship; a form of prayer or worship for special use.[1]

Unfortunately, in many Christian homes "having devotions" means exactly that—nothing more than a religious observance. But in my home growing up, and in our house today, we apply the word without the "s":

> Devotion: 1. profound dedication, consecration. 2. earnest attachment to a cause, person, etc.[2]

In our family we seek to be "profoundly dedicated" and "earnestly attached" to a person—Jesus Christ. A mere religious observance would simply never do for family devotions. It wouldn't suffice in the same way it wouldn't if, in seeking to know my child, I scheduled daily readings on the subject of her life. Or if in an attempt to stay devoted to my husband I recited a greeting to him every time he walked in the front door from work: "Dear Dave, I welcome you into our home once again to receive our bountiful but slightly burnt harvest meal as a reward for your faithful labor. Kindly remove your boots. Amen."

That is not to say we don't have a structured form of family devotions. I *love* my daily routine! But there is a lot of flexibility. In our home family devotions look much as they did when I was a kid. Mom and Dad understood how to apply Deuteronomy 11:19 to leading my siblings and me to a close relationship with God:

> Teach them [God's words] to your children, talking about them when you sit at home and when you walk along the road, when you lie down and when you get up.
> —DEUTERONOMY 11:19

Let's break up that verse into four parts and talk about what an authentic devotional life with our children might look like.

"When You Sit at Home..."

This presupposes that families will actually sit together at home. Studies show that families who eat meals together on a regular basis turn out kids who are far less likely to use drugs and who are physically and emotionally healthier.[3] But most studies don't point out that sitting around the dinner table as a family can also encourage the *spiritual* health of our children. If a hectic day doesn't allow for morning or evening devotions ("when you lie down" and "when you get up"), we can seize dinnertime as a great opportunity for spiritual discussion with our kids.

It helps to come to the table prepared. I have found that if I don't at least have a split-second plan for what we are going to talk about, our thirty precious supper minutes will be spent on militant policing of food pickiness, manners, or—at best—superficial babble (not that one shouldn't be concerned with pickiness or bad manners). So I try to think of something pertinent to recent family happenings or current events, for example, and make a life lesson out of it. If you feel you'd have to pull your brain out of the freezer in order to dream up dinnertime topics of conversation, have no fear! Here are a few suggestions, broken down by main topics, to get your creative juices flowing. Remember, keep it fun.

Church

- (For Mondays) What did you learn about in Sunday school yesterday?

- Can anyone tell me what the pastor preached about yesterday? (It would be a good idea to know the answer yourself.)

- What did you do in youth group last night?

- How can you be a better example of a worshipper for your peers at church?

- What would Jesus think if He watched you at church? Would He think you love Him based on the way you worship? Would your friends think you love Him?

- Why do we go to church?

- Do you like going to church (Sunday school, youth group)? Why or why not?

Politics and current events

- Does God want us to pray for our president?

- According to the Bible, what makes a good leader for a nation?

- Are we living in the last days? What are the signs, according to the Bible?

- What is going on in the world right now? How should we as a Christian family respond to this?

Relationships

- How are you kids getting along with one another?

- What can we do to be better parents?
  a. Give you Skittles cereal for breakfast
  b. Buy you an iPhone
  c. Let you drive to the store
  d. Teach you God's ways and show you His kind of love

- Is anyone bullying you at school? How would God (not Mom) want you to handle that?
  a. Pelt him with your BB gun
  b. Call him a "snot-nosed wart hog"
  c. Pray for him

      d. Tell your teacher and parents

      e. Two of the above

- Tell me about your teachers. Who is your favorite, and why?

- Who is your best friend? Why? Will he/she still be your best friend in twenty years? Why or why not?

- What kind of man (woman) should you marry?

      a. One with a dog

      b. One who is rich

      c. One who is rich and has a dog

      d. One who loves God with all his (her) heart

- Why is answer D important?

Finances

- Why does God bless some people with a lot of money?

      a. So they can buy an Xbox 360

      b. So they can give it all away

      c. So they can keep it under their mattress

      d. So they can advance God's kingdom by investing and giving to those in need, as God directs them

I am sure you can expand this list significantly. You may want to keep a small dry erase board on the fridge to jot down "things to talk about" as they come to mind. Or you can invest in the Ungame. It's a noncompetitive card game of questions that give rise to a "serious exchange of thoughts, feelings and ideas."[4] It comes in kids, teens, and families versions. Topics will surely surface that can be turned into spiritual discussion.

Here is an example of one of our most recent "when you sit down" times of family devotion: We'd been counting on receiving a sum of money in the mail for quite some time, and the whole family was aware of it. I'd made the sad mistake of causing my kids to hang all their hopes on getting this money. Every time they asked me for something, I'd say, "Wait until we get our check." I'd started my own personal list of things I was finally going to be able to buy when the magic envelope arrived in the mail. With Dave being unemployed in his field, we'd "made do" for a long time, and the hope of these coming funds was a light at the end of a long financial tunnel, and it kept me holding on to a superficial contentment.

But one evening Dave and I found out the money wouldn't be coming to us as soon as we'd previously been told. In fact, our wait might be significantly longer. Or the money might never arrive. I was disappointed but quickly adjusted my perspective, thanks to what I'd been learning through my own personal devotions and several years of practice in financial disappointment. But now I'd have to help my kids readjust.

During the following dinnertime Dave and I told our girls the news: our proverbial ship wasn't coming in after all. I apologized to the girls for instilling in them a false hope. I explained that I'd been wrong to let them believe the lie that we couldn't be completely happy until we had more money to buy more stuff. We talked about the blessing of learning contentment and how miserable many wealthy people are because they don't have what we have: health, love, and God. We ended that dinner conversation by memorizing Proverbs 15:17 together: "Better is a dinner of herbs where love is, than a fatted calf with hatred" (NKJV).

That time of "devotions" was as natural as, well, sitting down to supper and having a conversation! There was no boring study to read, no yawning faces to call back to attention. The kids were fully engaged and learned something I don't think they'll soon forget.

I do not mean to say that one should strive to converse on a deep level at every single meal. Some days we are tired, stressed, and need nothing more than "Talk Lite!" For those evenings I like to throw out my kids' favorite question, "What was the highlight of your day?", and leave it at that. If I forget, they remind me!

"Jesus Must Love Me!"

Today the main floor of the house is suffering from housekeeper's neglect. The carpet is strewn with Polly Pockets and cracker crumbs. Last night's unwashed pots and pans clamor for scour power.

The messy rooms beckon, but I choose to stick to the afternoon reading routine. Anna, Sarah, and I sink into the couch along with Friday night's popcorn kernels. I thumb through *The Lion, the Witch, and the Wardrobe* to find the chapter in which Aslan is killed. That is where we left off last.

Understanding dawns in my girls' eyes as I read about Aslan and the White Witch striking a bargain to let punishment-deserving Edmund go free. I sense their sorrow as Susan and Lucy follow their beloved lion friend through the midnight forest to the Stone Table.

There his devilish enemies bind and shear him, mocking and jeering at how lamblike the once fierce king of beasts has become.

My voice wavers as I read that Aslan could have easily bitten off a wolf's head while they muzzled him. How one great roar might have sent his torturers running. And about the damage that may have been done with one blow from his giant paw. But he didn't rescue himself.

I ask the girls why Aslan would allow such a thing. They understand he is giving himself over to the death that Edmund is due, according to the Law of the Deep Magic. Blood must be shed for the traitor to go free.

I close the book momentarily and look into the faces of my young daughters. "Girls, we are Edmund."

Six-year-old Anna gasps, looks at me wide-eyed, and whispers with sudden revelation, "Jesus must love me!"

She rests her head on my shoulder, reflecting. I notice the sunbeams streaming through the window and think about gardening chores lost to yet another afternoon spent indoors. My mind drifts back to the dirty bedrooms I could be transforming. The flashy achievements I won't soon realize.

I turn again to see my girls' watery, sober eyes as they consider Aslan . . . Jesus. How He loves them.

Quiet, you dusty shelves. Hush, you lofty ambitions. I am content in this moment. And most fulfilled.

—Faith Bogdan

"When You Walk Along the Road . . . "

We are talking about a lifestyle here. "Devotions"— learning the ways of God—shouldn't be confined to thirty minutes of Bible reading each morning or to a quaint prayer tower hidden atop a winding staircase above the attic (though that would be nice; come to think of it, I want one, right now). Dave and I are intentional about recognizing teachable moments with our kids throughout each day. These gems of opportunity can be found in the most unlikely places if we keep our eyes and ears open.

When Sarah was in junior high school, her social studies class was assigned to pick any current event, research it, and give an oral report on it to the class. She was overwhelmed with choices, so I suggested she present a topic rarely covered in mainstream media: the increasing persecution of Christians in some countries. She decided to report on what was happening in northern India: pastors' homes were being burned down and their families tortured, carried off to jail, or executed by Hindu militants. I coached her in being an objective reporter. She used the word *religious* in place of *Christian* and was careful to present only the facts. She wrote an article she could be proud of and read it aloud to her teacher and classmates the next day.

I sat there in her bedroom, observing her live, public school cyber class. Sarah was one of the last students to present, so we both had a chance to hear the teacher's reactions to the other kids' reports. Each one received an enthusiastic, "Bravo!" or "Nice job!" from the teacher. But after Sarah gave her presentation, the teacher responded with a disappointing, monotone, "Thank you." Sarah was crushed. My split-second instinct was to call the school and complain about discrimination. (We had, for weeks, already been getting vibes of intolerance from this teacher.)

But what would that have taught Sarah? That we should be surprised when people mistreat us because of our beliefs? That we should retaliate? Thankfully I was able to shift away from mother-bear emotions and seize the teachable moment. I reminded Sarah of Jesus's words to His disciples: "Blessed are those who are persecuted for righteousness' sake" (Matt. 5:10, NKJV). I told her that we should expect persecution, and we talked about the difference between being persecuted for "righteousness' sake" and for "being right's sake."

I explained that too many Christians are more interested in being right than in being righteous. If I had called the school principal and complained about discrimination on the part of the teacher, I would have had a case. I would have been right. And I would have no doubt brought on more undue persecution from the teacher. But that's not the kind of persecution Jesus blesses. The kingdom of heaven belongs to the righteous. So we prayed blessings for Sarah's teacher instead.

I told Sarah she'd received her "white belt" in handling persecution. This was only the beginning. Instances like these would follow her into adulthood and into the workplace for as long as she followed Jesus. It was better to start training now in how to properly respond to the cruelty of some people who reject our God.

Each of our days is a wealth of wisdom-treasures if we approach them with the pickaxe of intentionality in hand: "Tune your ears to wisdom....Cry out for insight, and ask for understanding. Search for them as you would for silver; seek them like hidden treasures" (Prov. 2:2–4, NLT).

To devote ourselves to seeking divine wisdom from everyday experiences is to fortify the character of our children with precious minerals from the Rock (Christ

Jesus). Rather than run from or shelter my children from the world, I see how God can make us more like Him through living in the world. So if Ruthie gets off the school bus and tells me about the girl who called her a mean name, I talk with her about what pain and losses that child might have to endure at home and how Ruthie can be her nurturer and not her victim.

Or when she asks whether or not the acquaintance I chat with at the store is a Christian, I say, "No, but isn't she nice?" And we discuss how every person is made in the image of God and is equally valued by Him while not discounting the need for that person's salvation. When Rebecca whines because she doesn't like stir-fry for dinner, I talk to her about the murmuring Israelites in the wilderness. When I'm helping Anna select a sensible brand of cupcake liners in the baking aisle, I teach her about godly stewardship of our finances and unit pricing. This is how we "walk along the road."

"When You Lie Down..."

My earliest memory of time spent with my mother was when she read to me at night from a two-volume set of Christian storybooks. I still remember the one about "Grumble Glasses," for example, and the kids who had to wear them every time they whined. I now own the nostalgic books with their fifties-style illustrations of mothers cooking in dresses and high heels.

I relish the hours spent reading to Ruthie and Rebecca from these books before bedtime. I want to give them the same memories my mother gave me. I also use *The Bible Story*—the popular blue, ten-volume set for the younger years. Why should I rely entirely on Sunday school to do what is my job as a parent—that is, to lead my kids to a personal relationship with God through the study of His Word?

As I've mentioned before, there is nothing rigorous about our family's lifestyle of devotion to God. I read to Ruthie and Rebecca as often as I can. This may be a quick fifteen-minute "date" with them while their two older sisters are finishing up the dinner dishes. It does not happen every night. Our main family devotion time involves three elements: reading aloud, Scripture memorization, and praying together as a family in the living room after dinner. Again, this is as we are able—usually a few times per week.

Reading

We pick books that will engage the wide age-range of listeners in our family while also teaching biblical truths. In our house it works out better for me to read and let Dave snuggle with the girls on the couch while they listen. We especially like inspiring, true stories of real heroes of the faith. Here are a few of our recent good reads:

- *Bruchko* (a story about a missionary to the Motilone Indians)[5]

- *Hinds' Feet on High Places* (an allegory and timeless classic about spiritual maturity; this is available in a children's version)[6]

- *Heaven Is for Real* (a young boy's account of his after-death visit to heaven)[7]

- *Jesus Freaks* (stories of historical and present-day Christian martyrs)[8]

- *I'll Cross the River* (true-to-life story of religious persecution in northern Korea)[9]

- *Frida: Chosen to Die, Destined to Live* (the true story of a Rwandan genocide survivor)[10]

- *The Chronicles of Narnia: The Lion, the Witch, and the Wardrobe* (a clear portrayal of the gospel)[11]

Scripture memorization

Memorizing the Scriptures is important to Dave and me at a time in history in which the possibility of Bibles being outlawed in an increasingly secularized America is easier to imagine than it was when he and I were kids. Dad paid me one dollar per verse to memorize Scripture. Some may criticize his method as a form of bribery and sacrilege. But the truth is, thirty-some years later, I can still recite those chapters I memorized for money. They are my "sleeping pills" on nights when I'm troubled and an emotional anchor for trying moments as a mom. Those verses course through my mind at times and keep me from sinking into pits of despair, and they have served as "duct tape" to save me from countless relational mishaps. "I have stored up your word in my heart, that I might not sin against you" (Ps. 119:11, ESV).

At present, Anna and Sarah have memorized the following chapters of the Bible: Psalm 23, Psalm 91, Matthew 5, John 15, and 1 Corinthians 13 ($142.00 worth!). Ruthie and Rebecca are learning single verses. After our read-aloud time we either review some of the scriptures we've memorized, or we work on new chapters or verses. My girls readily assume the task of checking me for mistakes as I quote passages. Perhaps it's due to my habit of replacing words now and then to see if they're still listening: "Blessed are they which do hunger and thirst after vegetables..."

I admit, this requires discipline on Dave's and my part. Some nights I'm tired and Dave has fallen asleep on the couch, and the last thing we want to do is work on Scripture memorization. I try to focus on Sarah's sweet voicing of Psalm 103 (our current endeavor), but my mind drifts to the awaiting pillow upstairs. Other nights I simply don't want to have "devotions." I'm tempted to rush through it so that Dave and I can get on with our planned evening of Netflix and Nutella. Still, this is one area that we believe is too important to let slide. And yet again, we don't want our kids to end up hating it. So there's flexibility and grace, and sometimes a movie with a great spiritual parallel is the order of the day.

Prayer

Our evening devotions always conclude with praying together. We simply remind each other of what needs we or others have and bring them before God. Dave and I encourage the girls to start their prayers with thanksgiving for specific blessings. I am continually amazed at the willingness of our girls to pray aloud. We rarely have to coax them. One by one they offer up the sweetest, heartfelt prayers. The most memorable one was when Anna, at age thirteen, prayed this: "Dear Lord, thank You that although Dad doesn't have a job right now, You have provided all that we need and more. Thank You for taking such good care of us." Her voice cracked with emotion at the end of the prayer, and my heart flip-flopped with joy at all the things my daughter was learning in life— including how to pray.

"When You Get Up..."

I'm convinced it was the daily, early-morning talks with my dad over an open Bible that got me through high school with my purity, good grades, and salvation still intact. Those devotional times never felt forced or sounded like a lecture. Dad would simply open the Bible— say, to Proverbs—and expound on a verse or two for as long as it took me to finish my muesli. He applied what he read to my life—to my school friends, teachers, and boyfriends; to my studies and career goals; to my self-esteem. God's Word came alive through my dad's lips. He helped me understand who God is and what He's like— both through the opening of the Scriptures and by just being there for me every day. I cherished those times at the snack bar with Victor Dodzweit, and if I've gained any wisdom at all in life, I owe much of it to those morning devotions with Dad. He was a very busy man, in full-time business and ministry, but I felt like I was a priority every day before I left for school.

I've tried to replicate that model with my own teen-agers. These days, before Anna's and Sarah's cyber classes start each morning, I call them to the living room where we continue our current journey through the four Gospels. I don't have a reading schedule; I place no demands on myself for how much of the New Testament we'll get through within a certain amount of time. In my opinion this quality time with my teens is too sacred to rush through with man-made guidelines. So we simply pick up where we left off the last time. We read a small section of Scripture and discuss it together. Sometimes there is enough "meat" in a few verses to "chew" on for a while. I try to prevent spiritual indigestion by cramming too much down their throats at a time.

If it's a morning in which we simply don't get to devotions due to a late night before, an appointment, or whatever, I don't sweat it. Our devotional time is about knowing God and feeding our spirits through His Word. This should not involve guilt for the same reason that I don't feel guilt when I skip a meal; I feel *hunger.*

Devotional observances in some families involve enforcing a strict crack-of-dawn schedule in which blurry-eyed kids nod off while potentially life-changing words are being read and wasted. I respect parents who go that route. But family devotions in our home are like a daily Christmas. God's wisdom is waiting for us like packages to unwrap, not chores to check off a to-do list.

I'm not saying my teens relish every minute of devotions. They meet with me on the sofa before school starts because they have a healthy "fear of Mom." But they know that the minute I recognize a hardening of their souls, in the way they sometimes stare out the window and refuse to respond, I'll shut the Bible, put my arms around them, and say, "What can I do to be a better mom?" *Because I have come to understand that when a child distances herself from a parent, it is often because the parent has first distanced herself from the child through being too busy or too much a nag.*

And if there is a hindrance in my kids' relationship with me, how can I expect to ever encourage their relationship with God? So I lay aside "devotions" in order to devote myself to my daughters for a while, holding them close and letting them hear my prayer: "Lord, please help me to be a better mother. Forgive me for being so impatient. Show me creative ways to spend more time with my precious girls."

The natural result of this heart-devotion is that Anna, Sarah, Rebecca, and Ruthie will be drawn, by God's grace, back to the Bible, time and time again, to learn more about this God who humbles their mother to listen carefully to the voice of the Holy Spirit. That voice is what helps us distinguish religious duty from an authentic pursuit of relationship.

 Refrigerator Magnet: Devotion to God is a way of life, not a religious ritual.

 Heart Exam: What small step can I take today to turn my children's faces toward eternity?

Chapter 12

JUST SAY YES TO FUN!

A PARENTING MAGAZINE WAS running a contest in which kids could draw a picture of themselves having fun with their mom. The grand prize was a Wii. I encouraged the girls to enter the contest and couldn't wait to see all the wonderful ideas they would come up with for drawings. I passed out extra sheets of sturdy paper (they were sure to have multiple ideas) and spread my special scrapbooking pens around the table for my little artists' project.

"OK, girls, start drawing! What have we done together that's fun?"

Silence.

"C'mon girls, there's got to be *something* we do for fun. What do you like to do with me?"

They looked at one another, one rolled her eyes, and another rested her head on the table, yawning. Finally one of them confessed, "We don't do anything fun with you."

I fell onto a chair and looked at each one of my daughters, processing their verdict. Nothing fun? Didn't we read together every day? I homeschooled, for crying out loud! We had lively dinner discussions. Wasn't I the Queen of Family Togetherness?

I asked my kids what things they would consider "fun,"

and they rattled off their ideas. It was then that I realized I was not the mom of their dreams. They were half raised—a few short years from leaving the nest—and had no pictures to draw. The contest was suddenly about more than winning a Wii.

In the days that followed I worked hard at being fun. I played baseball with Sarah. (I hit the ball so far, I stood gawking at it instead of running to base. She tagged me out.) I had a "trampoline date" with Ruthie. I have a treasured, permanent mental image of her little six-year-old frame flopping up and down like a rag doll, squealing with delight as I bounced her high into the air. A week later she was still telling people about the day she jumped on the trampoline "with just Mommy." I invested in Apples to Apples, a game of which Rebecca became the champion. I taught Anna to bake.

But the baseball was left by the edge of the pond to gather algae and now blends in with the bulrushes. My aging bones groan with each bounce on that hard trampoline. Card games get old, and Anna no longer needs me to help her bake. Days come and go, replacing my good intentions with blank memories and disappointment in myself for failing at "fun." I feel the underlying panic of kids growing too tall and too heavy and too old and too independent to need mommy-entertainment; the years are a blur of fast-fading memories.

My baby is nine; there are but a few tomorrows left to play.

Make "Mom-Fun" Time

A wise woman named Barbara Tennant once came to our MOPS (Mothers of Preschoolers International) group and presented a slideshow called "Just Say Yes." It was a series of photos she'd taken of instances in which she'd chosen to say yes to requests her kids had made that might evoke an immediate "No!" from the average busy mom. She'd said yes to questions such as:

- "Mom, can we have a picnic in the trunk of the car?"
- "Can we put the entire bottle of dish soap in the wading pool?"
- "Can I give baby brother a ride in the back of my toy pickup truck?"
- "Can we camp out in the back of dad's truck tonight?"
- "Can we watch TV on our heads?"
- "Can we take all the sand in the sandbox and stuff it down our shirts?"
- "Can we play in the new load of topsoil?"
- "Can I make a sandwich out of whatever I want, all by myself?"

I'd been a part of MOPS for over a decade, and as Barb talked about the need to have fun with our children, I couldn't recall seeing women cry and as much mascara run in any meeting as it did that day. It's because we moms know we're falling short here. My own creativity level in this area was zero. I needed a plan.

If you feel that way too, I'd like to offer you a few of my favorite tried-and-true ideas for fun activities to do with your kids. (Use common sense in determining which age groups each of these work best with.) There are some additional related resources listed in the back of this book. You may be inspired with creative "Mom-Fun" activities of your own by the end of this chapter!

Give mom a makeover

Invest in dollar-store makeup for the sole purpose of turning your kids into your own beauty consultants. Now that mine are getting older, they actually apply makeup on the part of my face it was intended for! (Note: You may want to consider washing your face before answering the door or going out in public if your makeup artists are especially young.) This activity doesn't get old. My teenagers still love doing my makeup! If you have boys and applying makeup to mom's face is not high on their priority list, purchase some clown makeup instead.

Turn up the music and dance

Never underestimate the power of five dancing minutes in the kitchen to lighten everyone's mood. (Note: If your kids scream and run away when you start dancing—as mine do—it is because they are simply overcome at the sheer impressiveness of your moves. Trust me on this.)

Read books in strange places

I once threw a couple of large comforters over the dining table and huddled under it with the kids as we read *Where the Wild Things Are* by flashlight. What made the experience extra special was the sound effects track of howling wolves on the CD I played in the background. We have also read books together in piles of leaves, snow forts (with a thermos of hot cocoa), the attic, and under the Christmas tree. The possibilities are endless!

Browse photo albums

This is perhaps my favorite way to spend time with my kids at any age. There is no preparation or cleanup involved. We simply dig out one of our family photo albums and snuggle on the couch or in "strange places" for a good while of reminiscing. We often rediscover forgotten fun activities this way.

Doll or car wash

Give your child a huge mixing bowl of sudsy water and a rag, and let him/her wash all the plastic dolls or cars in the toy box. This is a great warm-weather activity to do outside or in a bathtub during colder months.

Scavenger hunt

Give each child a recyclable plastic bag and a list of things to find on a nature walk. Items might include a pine cone, a piece of fern, an acorn, a bird feather, a toad-stool, birch bark, a dandelion, a wild berry, a spider web (which can be left intact), some green or Spanish moss (depending on where you live), and so on. Kids especially love to team up and compete to see who can find all the items on the list first. Have a prize ready! This activity has been a great motivator for getting my girls out the door for fresh air and exercise when they'd rather be cleaning their room. Except that has never been the case.

Gardening

If you're like me and would rather be reading than weeding, consider starting a potted herb garden on the patio. Kids love helping in the kitchen if they can snip plants they have helped to grow. A child as young as two can start seeds in an egg carton filled with potting soil.

Make play dough together

This recipe can be made within five minutes and lasts for months in a sealed container stored in the fridge:

> 1 cup flour
> ½ cup salt
> 1 cup water
> 2 Tbsp. oil
> 2 Tbsp. cream of tartar
>
> Mix the dry stuff in a saucepan, add the wet, and stir over medium heat until it forms a ball. Let it cool, and knead in a few drops of food coloring. You may separate the dough into a few pieces for making different colors.[1]

Play dough birds' nests

A garlic press doubles as a fabulous tool for creating play dough hair, spaghetti, or anything stringy. My girls made birds' nests using yellow play dough and my garlic press. Then they shaped blue play dough into small eggs.

Play dough porcupines

One time I gave Sarah a ball of play dough and a handful of uncooked spaghetti, broken in halves. I instructed her to make a "porcupine" by poking each noodle piece into the dough. I gave her two small seashell noodles for the eyes. She loved it.

Make slime together

When it's back-to-school time, I stock up on twenty-cent bottles of Elmer's glue sold at Walmart. I buy a box of Borax, which can be found with the laundry detergent and costs only two or three dollars. Here is my favorite slime recipe:

> Stir and dissolve 1 tsp. of Borax into a cup of water. In a separate container, mix ½ cup of white glue with ½ cup of water. Add food coloring if you desire. Then combine the two solutions and watch them transform into slime.[2]

If you are the homeschooling type, you may want to let this art project double as a science lesson about polymers. I would explain polymerization here, but my chemist husband would surely scrutinize my efforts since I once told the kids the elemental symbol for gold is "Or." I was confusing it with Orion, which I momentarily believed to be the bear constellation. But it turns out I was thinking of *oro* (Spanish for gold) and *oso* (Spanish for bear). You have to admit, I have something in the language department. But my husband has never since allowed me to teach chemistry to the children.

While I am shamelessly confessing my weakness in some areas of science, I should let you know that I gave Rebecca homemade green slime for Christmas one year—a spider clipart label on a Chinese takeout soup container, the slime replete with plastic spiders I'd purchased around Halloween. *She* thought I was brilliant.

Easy pizzas

Combine an art project with meal planning by giving your child a pita round, some pizza sauce, and toppings. Let him spread on the sauce and decorate the pita. Pop it in the oven and voilà! Lunch is served.

Trace your child's body

Purchase a roll of finger paint paper and have your child lie down on a stretch of it and let you trace his body. Then he can design "himself" with crayons, markers, or paint, and hang his full-body poster in his room. For a really fun twist, let him trace and decorate Mom!

Apple and orange sponge painting

This classic kindergarten craft never gets old; even Martha Stewart, I'm sure, has been known to cut apples and oranges in half, dip the halves in paint, and blot fabric with them (and get paid thousands of dollars for doing it). Kids can use washable paint and paper. Cut the apples different ways to show the star shape of the core or the butterfly shape of the apple half.

Paint a house

Pick up a discarded appliance box from a home improvement store and cut out windows and a door. Let your child paint his own castle or barn. Be sure to tell the dog that this is *not* a place to pee. I have reason to offer this advice.

Play wolf hunt

Make your space pitch-dark. Have everyone get down on all fours (it's safer that way, lessening the chance of nose-ramming and body-slamming) and, without making a noise, prowl about in search of others. When you bump into someone, snicker quietly, and stay with them and wait to be discovered by someone else. The game ends when the "wolf" left alone finds the pack. (Note for when two parents are involved: Kids love the thrill and suspense of hunting in the dark, but they don't necessarily appreciate finding Mom and Dad kissing in a corner, having forgotten about the game. Don't be surprised if the light switch is suddenly flipped on and the kids groan, "Not again!")

Build a giant spider web

Give your children a skein of yarn and some scissors, and let them create their own giant spider web by tying, winding, and stretching lengths of yarn from and around parts of furniture and sturdy objects. The result is a human-sized web that can fill up the space of a room and give kids lots of fun maneuvering their way through it. We did this in our recreation room where the potential for property damage was minimal and left it up for several days.

Play the "Stories" game

This is a family favorite of ours and works great with older kids, providing an excellent opportunity to practice the basics of good story-writing skills. Give each family member a sheet of notebook paper and a writing utensil. Have everyone write a one-sentence opening to a story at the top of the paper. Then each player should pass his paper to the person on his left and add a sentence to the paper passed to them. Then fold the paper down from the top, covering *only the previous sentence.* Papers are again passed clockwise, and each person adds a sentence to the previous one, which should be the only sentence visible. As papers are passed around and new sentences added, the stories begin to take interesting twists and turns. The passing of papers is finished when each player reaches the bottom of the page. Then the fun really begins! Each player unfolds his piece of paper and reads aloud what has become an entire story. Expect lots of laughs and silly storylines!

Home spa

Building on the makeup idea mentioned previously, why not gather the raw materials you have in your cabinets and cupboards and create a home spa? Make massage oil by adding a few drops of your favorite extract or essential oil to some mild olive oil. Just be sure not to confuse your oils and use this one in your pizza dough! (My friend and fellow writer Torry Martin once accidentally polished his furniture with generic butter spray, for your information. But that wasn't nearly as bad as discovering he'd coated his griddle with furniture polish, after wondering, for months, why his pancakes tasted like lemon.)

Foot massages are a great way to connect with the child whose "love language" is physical touch. (I can only speak as a mom with all girls here. You know your child and how he feels about people touching his tootsies.) For an unforgettable pedicure that won't deplete your bank account or even drag you out of the comfort of home, start out with a luxurious salt or sugar scrub: Mix one part oil (olive, vegetable, or baby oil is fine) with two parts salt or sugar. Add five drops of an essential oil if you wish. Stir and store in an airtight container. (I use sugar, vegetable oil, and a little vanilla extract.)

Massage between toes and into soles and heels and watch your child melt! (If you rub deep enough, you might even awaken your inner reflexologist and discover a disease. I know this because one such practitioner once dug into my Achilles tendon and, when I yelped in pain, diagnosed pockets in my colon.) Finally, wipe the scrub off with a warm, wet washcloth and massage a yummy-scented lotion into the feet. Seal pedicure with a kiss to the toes. When we do a spa day, I play soft music and light candles to set the mood and make the experience extra special. Major brownie points for Mom!

Treasure hunt

I had a blast with this recently. First, I made the "treasure." I filled a fancy gift box with a few items from my "gift stash" (because I have girls I used cheap "body butter," makeup samples, a small craft kit, etc.) and some goodies I sacrificed from my private chocolate stash. Then I grabbed a writing tablet, the treasure, and headed out the door to write clues and hide the treasure after making sure the girls were secured inside for a while. We have thirty-two wooded acres, so the added bonus to this activity was that I got my exercise! But don't feel you have to have that much room; in fact, you can do this indoors.

The fun for me was writing the clues. Kids love to think they're solving a mystery, so try to be as poetic and metaphorical as possible. (Or don't. Just have fun.) As I walked through the woods, I wrote directions leading to where I'd ultimately leave the treasure. Some of them were:

- "Walk the plank." (Walk across the fallen tree trunk. They told me later that their favorite part of the adventure was having to do certain things along the way that didn't even relate to finding the treasure.)

- "Return the golden ring." (Put the round, orange sled you left in the yard back under the porch where it belongs. Never before had I seen four kids fight over who gets to do a chore.)

You can even incorporate Scripture memorization into your treasure hunt. I used "Narrow is the way," and for the final clue, "Where your treasure is, there will your 'art' be also." (I tacked a piece of Sarah's artwork to the tree trunk in which the treasure was hidden.)

To make the treasure hunt "professional," I quickly typed up the clues before going out with the girls on the treasure hunt. I used a bold, gothic font. They were so impressed they dressed up as squires to fit the occasion.

Letterboxing and "geocaching"

These two pastimes are similar in nature, as they both involve going online to get information for finding real-world treasure outdoors. If you are like me and still live in the dark ages when it comes to technology, you may not own a GPS. (And frankly, the voice in that devise is misguided. I borrowed a GPS once and considered throwing it out the window because she didn't apologize for getting me lost.) At any rate, you'll need a GPS for geocaching. When I finally get one, I plan to join the millions of geocachers out there.

This game is right up my alley—for the exercise, exploration, adventure, intrigue, and, yes, fun time spent with my kids. Basically you go to the official Geocaching website (geocaching.com) and, using geographical coordinates, locate a "geocache"—a container that someone has filled with a treasure and hidden (there are over a million geocaches out there). You can also share your geocaching experiences with the online community of fellow treasure hunters.

Letterboxing is the old-fashioned version of geocaching (it has been around since the 1800s). Instead of using a GPS, you go to an online letterboxing website (yes, they had the Internet back then) and find clues to the location of a local "treasure," which in this case is a rubber stamp that someone has made and a paper tablet. I like this activity because of the artwork involved; you can create your own unique rubber stamp to bring along. When you find the "letterbox," use your stamp in that person's tablet (date it and perhaps leave a message) and stamp your own tablet with the stamp you find. That way you're keeping a record of all the letterboxes you have found (thus documenting your adventures) while leaving a trace of yourself behind for others to enjoy.

You never know where a letterboxing expedition will take you. One time the girls and I ended up at a monastery outside of town and got to explore a crypt and eat fresh-picked plums offered by a monk. Like the treasure hunt I created for my girls, the clues to a letterbox are often poetic and mysterious ("Walk forty paces toward the hunch-back tree"), making the adventure all the more spectacular.

Bring Them Into Your World

Ultimately kids just want to be with Mom doing *anything.* There are no ground rules for how spending time with your children should look. Do not for a second feel guilty if you don't get down on the floor and play with Barbies or LEGOs. But do bring your kids into your everyday life. It doesn't have to always be playing, per se. Try letting them enter into your grown-up world.

For instance, the minute my girls were old enough to appreciate the value of a penny, I paid them one cent per item to fold a basket of washcloths. Pretty soon they graduated to towels and matching socks. They thought they were "big time," and their piggy banks filled up. Those were precious times, sitting on the floor with them, teaching them how to fold and stack. See? No *Family Fun* magazine needed—I simply brought them into my moment-by-moment living. Eventually I stopped paying them to fold laundry; it became one of the household chores expected of those who like to eat and have a warm place to sleep.

Some moms enjoy baking with their kids, and I am not one of them. Well, not when they're two. Not when they're fighting with their sisters over the chair and pushing one another off and crumbling eggshells into the mixing bowl and creating a hurricane of flour and batter-splatter with the hand mixer. These are not precious memories in my book. My hat goes off to those very patient mothers who can bake with the toddler propped up on the counter, unfazed by her attempts to slather chocolate frosting on her hair.

But if you're like me, feel free to put off culinary school for your little ones until they are bigger ones. No one is going to call Child Protective Services on you. I have finally reached the stage in which Ruthie is old enough to help me in the kitchen without me pulling my hair out. I thoroughly enjoy these times together. She loves to peel garlic and grate cheese, and she now knows how to make the perfect fried egg all by herself—hers are even better than mine.

I try to include the kids in as much as possible. I wonder if, by waiting for official "play times" with our kids, we can easily miss those tiny, golden moments of together-ness that are just as meaningful. I have found that a few minutes of Internet browsing (if it must be done) can be a great snuggle date with whoever happens to be within reach. I'll grab her, make room on my La-Z-Boy and say, "What do you think of these binoculars?" Or, "How does this recipe sound? Let's see what the reviewers say." Or, "Take a look at the news page with me. Let's see what's going on in the world." Or, "I wonder if I can roast a turkey on Speed Bake."

These moments of togetherness are invaluable. Whatever gets done in the meantime is secondary. Sure, you found the perfect Hungarian goulash recipe. You got in on the eBay bidding for a great pair of Nikon binoculars at a third the retail price. You learned about convection cooking. But while you were getting those things done, you were holding that little munchkin as tightly as you could without squashing her, smoothing back her hair and whispering sweet nothings in her ear as you clicked that mouse. And you know what? Not only does your child now know how to search for a recipe and what the eye of a hurricane looks like, but she also knows Mom loves her enough to draw her in and treat her as someone worthy to teach, and worthy to love, every minute.

 Refrigerator Magnet: Love is spelled T-I-M-E.

 Heart Exam: Will my kids someday remember me as a mom who was busy—or fun?

Chapter 13

I'M SO LONELY!

I REMEMBER THE DAYS in which I'd watch the phone, trying to will it to ring. But we all know that a watched phone never rings, especially if it belongs to a lonely stay-at-home mom of tiny kids. Sometimes we are hurting too much to reach out—to pick up the phone and press buttons. We need someone else to do the reaching.

There was a relentless lack of adult conversation during my early years of motherhood, especially when Dave worked sixty-plus hours per week running his own business, often traveling far away from home. I'd go from room to room picking up toys and clothes, often crying quietly, wishing I had someone to talk to on a deeper level than "wipe your nose" and "pass the ketchup."

I remember trying to potty train my kids and feeling clueless and helpless. I'd convinced myself I had no friends. So I turned to the one friend I knew I could count on. I found myself lying prostrate on the floor one afternoon, hugging my box of tissues, venting in God's ear:

"I don't know what I'm doing, and I have no one to talk to. Will You please show me how to potty train this child? I'm tired of poop smeared into the carpet and yellow puddles on the floor. You said to ask for wisdom, so I'm asking. Oh, and I'm lonely. Will You please give me a friend?"

Psalm 62:8 says, "Confide in him at all times, ye people; pour out your heart before him: God is our refuge" (DARBY). My prayers didn't end with that conversation on the floor. I'd speak my mind, and then listen for a while, like any decent friend would. And without fail God would answer by wrapping me in an indescribable peace and a feeling of warmth that would draw more tears, this time of joy. Sometimes, I'd "hear" a practical word of wisdom: *When she's ready to potty train, it will be easy.* But mostly He'd respond with palpable love.

I don't remember if God answered my prayer for a friend right away. I still have blurred remains of ink-scribbled notes alongside key verses in the margins of my worn Bible that read, "Praying for a friend, 2/00." Maybe God wanted me to cultivate a better friendship with *Him* for a while.

It often takes hardship to fully understand what it means to be "hugged" by God. It is in "the valley of the shadow of death" that we feel the Shepherd's rod and staff of comfort (Ps. 23). Something about desperation creates a keen awareness of my need for God and of His presence that I don't find on the mountaintops—not that God isn't with me there too. It's just that when I'm sopped in my own happiness, I don't often sense a real longing to run into God's arms.

Research shows that "mothers with children at home are at a higher risk of suffering from depression than childless women and empty-nesters."[1] Of course, much of this depression is the result of loneliness. Carla Anne Coroy, author of *Married Mom, Solo Parent*, got so lonely as a young stay-at-home mom that she found herself searching the yellow pages for a live person to chat with about *anything.*

The ad for a paint and wallpaper store grabbed her attention: "Call us to talk about it!" So she did. She called and talked with one sales associate after another about home décor—not that she was interested in redecorating her house; she was willing to be put on hold and transferred from one adult voice to another in a desperate attempt to keep herself sane, all the while wondering if the odd phone call was itself a mark of insanity.[2]

I never thought of calling a paint store to fulfill my need for adult conversation when my kids were small. But I do remember hopping into the car and driving into town just to be surrounded by people within my age bracket. I'd stroll through the grocery store hoping to see someone I knew, wishing I was brave enough to at least strike up an honest exchange with the cashier. "Hi, I'm Lonely. How are you?"

But I was never that brave, and my side of the checkout counter remained woefully silent. God is changing that, with my cooperation.

I Have Issues

I think we each have our issues that keep us from reaching out for friendship. One of mine (besides living several miles removed from civilization) is in the area of cooking. I have a mental block about it. In theory I know that people really couldn't care less what I serve them for dinner; they crave conversation more than good food. But I still sometimes worry that what I feed them might not be "good enough." I wish I could be one of those snappy

Rachael Ray types who can whip up a fabulous casserole from a can of corn and a box of crackers.

My friend Carla Anne wasn't worried about that. I remember taking the kids to her house one day for a play date at lunchtime. She opened her kitchen cupboard and mused, "Let's see...I have a can of cream of mushroom soup. We can heat that up for lunch." I was enormously impressed at her confidence and touched by the fact that she trusted me as a friend who wouldn't judge her for not "having it together." I'd heard about the couples' Valentine's party she'd held in her unfurnished living room: guests brought picnic baskets and blankets for a romantic, candlelight dinner on the floor. They raved about it for weeks afterward. Why couldn't I be like that?

I have no excuse, really. My mom was the queen of hospitality (which, Carla Anne taught me, is very different from mere entertainment). She never cared what anyone thought of her cooking. She served burnt taco shells once to an old bachelor named Hobart Peel. He didn't mind letting Mom know that the shells reminded him of the potsherds Job used to scrape his boils. Mom laughed and scheduled the next dinner party. Somehow that particular carefree gene bypassed me.

I'm a decent cook; I can create a handsome plate of grilled salmon, squeaky-fresh green beans, and new potatoes with parsley. I know real food when I see it, and I like to serve it. But if it's out of my means, I sadly allow the budget to hinder my social life. I need to learn to do what my friend Suzette does: practice the art of potluck. I provide the house; friends provide the dinner. I'm working on that one, with an eye toward community, like the early church modeled: "Every day they continued to meet together.... They broke bread in their homes and ate together with glad and sincere hearts" (Acts 2:46).

Friendship: Step Across the Borders

Speaking of Suzette, let me tell you about one of my dearest friends and how I met her. I had taken the kids to the playground one day to swing while I watched from a bench. I was feeling lonely as usual. A woman pushed a jogging stroller past me on the bike path. My instinct was to run to her and say, "Do you need a friend? 'Cause I do." But I worried, "What if she's a snob? What if she's in a hurry? What if she wants to be left alone? What if she thinks I'm weird? What if I *am* weird?"

So I let her walk on by. I had a sinking feeling. "Why am I such an idiot?" I wondered. "Worst case scenario, she looks at me and says, 'Leave me alone, creep.' Nothing lost." I promised myself and God that I would befriend the next person who walked across the park lawn. Suzette appeared within five minutes, accompanying two kids—a boy and girl—both with long, flowing hair. Maybe it was her black-rimmed glasses or that they were feeding the squirrels, but something told me many promising conversations accompanied this potential friendship. Here was my second chance! But what would I say? I looked down, thinking, and noticed my bare wrist. I hadn't worn my watch. So I used that as an excuse to mosey over and ask if she knew the time.

Six years later Suzette is someone I can count on to be there on days I need to break out of the cabin and make sure life still exists beyond the woods. I coast down the hill and find my place on the couch at Nectar Floral Studio, where Suzette and I laugh away the day's stress or bare our souls as flowers nod fragrant sympathy. Ours is a rare friendship between two individuals with differing worldviews.

Suzette and I have too much in common to base our search for meaningful relationships on our individual religious belief systems. We are both moms who would die for our kids. We think similarly about their health and education; we both homeschool and prefer herbs over pills, books over TV. We value community. We may vote differently, but we are equally fierce in our pursuit of liberty and justice for all. Our idea of a family movie night is crowding around a computer screen to watch an online documentary or indie film. We despise greed and materialism and can't live without culture, art, and *real* food. We are both deeply spiritual yet vastly different in ways that commonly prevent people from pursuing this type of friendship.

Befriending across the borders of faith, politics, culture, and lifestyle is an ongoing education and adventure full of joy and wonder. To illustrate: One hot summer day I took my kids and Suzette's kids to the creek for a swim. At one point my girls came over to inform me that one of Suzette's children was eating minnows—swallowing them whole, live and wiggly, straight out of the murky water. I didn't have a cell phone to call for help, so I forced myself to keep calm and watch for signs of Sudden Live-Fish-Eating Death Syndrome. Nothing. The kids continued to splash about, and I decided reporting the child's dietary indiscretion could wait until I saw Suzette later that afternoon.

"I have to tell you something," I said, searching Suzette's eyes, already mentally planning fund-raiser dinners to cover the kid's hospital bills for the parasitic infestation sure to manifest itself that evening. "Your child ate several live minnows today. I couldn't stop it in time. I'm so sorry."

Suzette laughed, called the kid over, and said, "You should let the poor little creatures live!"

I wonder how many moms are isolated and lonely simply because they are afraid to "step across the borders" in seeking out friendship. Or they misunderstand the purpose in doing so. This is especially true among evangelical Christian moms. Well-meaning ministers sometimes do us a disservice in the way they teach evangelism, projecting the idea that all our day-to-day conversations should be driven—not by the desire to get to know the individual, but by an agenda to lead someone to repeat the sinner's prayer by day's end.

While I desperately want my friends and family in heaven with me, we are defeating Jesus's purpose in coming if we turn people off with our misguided agendas. We've bought into a "we versus them" mentality that the nonreligious can sniff out from across a room. In the eyes of many people, Christians are on the planet to fix others, whether they ask to be fixed or not. The religious are only interested in getting people to join their "club" (church) and become like them. When we consider this common perception, we should honestly ask ourselves why non-Christians would want to befriend us.

The other misconception among many in the church is that "worldly" people are spiritually dirty in a way that might defile us by spending time in their company. Yet

Jesus never had that concern. He never said, "I've got to get out of this dark town with all its bad influences." "I can't hang with Matthew; his greed might rub off on Me." "Mary is going to corrupt me if I spend too much time with her."

To the contrary, Jesus was drawn to these places and sought out friendships with not just the nonreligious but also with the town drunks and people of questionable reputation—so much so that the church people of the day accused Him of being one of them: "And when the Pharisees saw this, they said to his disciples, 'Why does your teacher eat with tax collectors and sinners?'" (Matt. 9:11, ESV).

Why did He do this? Why did Jesus cross borders? Because He loved them. Love was His driving passion in seeking out relationships with all kinds of people. And salvation was the end result of His kind of love. If we are to have any kind of agenda with people, it should be to love them. Not to preach to or convert them (that's the Holy Spirit's job), but to listen to their stories. To appreciate where they're coming from and understand why they believe the things they believe.

If we stick to a love agenda, the end result is much more likely to be salvation than it would be if we set out to change a person's worldview. Actually, it is at best ignorant and at worst arrogant to think it is our duty to upturn the entire belief system of a free-thinking individual. Would we expect anyone to so easily do that with us?

I am not by any means suggesting we hide under a "bushel" (Matt. 5:15). I have friends who are openly curious about my Bible-God and seek to pick my brain on the matter. I've spent many glorious hours having heart-to-heart talks about God with friends in the comfort of my living room or in a downtown café. And I've watched them, like hatchlings, begin to peck away at the shell of unbelief and emerge to new life.

The truth is, if we are wholehearted followers of Christ, we will in turn make more followers ("disciples") of Christ naturally through authentic and loving relationship. That includes treating others *and their beliefs* with utmost respect.

In fact, *I believe if we don't feel we have as much to learn from nonbelievers as they do from us, we need a dramatic shift in our thinking before we seek out their friendship.* I have learned enough from Suzette to fill an entirely different book (and I think I will). Because of her influence I have grown in huge ways as a person and, I hope, have become a more likable human being and, I dare say, one who is more pleasing to God.

Through our friendship I have learned to pause on life's busy highway and let myself be captivated by the wonder of God's creation, to savor ordinary moments, to value community more, to treasure natural resources and be resourceful myself, and to recognize beauty in everything, every person, and every place, including my small town of Elmira, New York. It's a place I considered uncultured and gone-to-seed until I began to meet other artsy residents through Suzette and caught their enthusiasm for downtown, where they are literally planting new seeds of hope in an economically depressed city and giving me newfound gratitude for living in the brush of its outskirts.

Respect Means "No Trespassing"

A love agenda—on *anyone's* part—intuitively knows if there is a "welcome sign" posted in the faith window of the relationship—an invitation to share one's spiritual beliefs. But a wise person also recognizes a "no trespassing sign" and respects it—and keeps on loving, no matter what.

Think about that, and put yourself in the shoes of a person who thinks the Bible is full of fairy tales and the idea of a talking snake in a tree or a man-swallowing fish is absurd. Now imagine a friend of yours is trying earnestly to convince you that aliens will be invading your garage next Thursday. If you are a person of reasonable intelligence, the "no trespassing sign" is going to be raised, and you will stand by your right to dismiss the alien story and believe your friend is sadly misguided. You will *not* appreciate your friend's mission to persuade you otherwise.

Crossing the borders with a love agenda means that if I suddenly saw into my friend's future and knew that she would never convert under my watch—that the "no trespassing sign" would permanently adhere to the faith window—*nothing changes in our friendship.* I cherish her for life. That doesn't mean I'm not taking long walks every day and crying out to God for her soul, begging Him to get her attention, as any true Christian friend would do.

It also means I have the freedom to be who I am with her—to talk naturally (not obnoxiously and incessantly, and *not* in any way contrived) about my faith and share my God-stories without the fear that she may suspect a religious agenda. And if I truly don't have one, everything runs smoothly and transparently between us.

Do you have a Suzette in your life? Christian or not, do you have that "someone" you can pour out your soul to and receive unconditional friendship based on trust, mutual respect, and love? If not, maybe a trip to the playground is in order.

Friendliness 101

Besides shying away from getting to know those of different religious and philosophical persuasions, another reason (perhaps the main reason) people remain lonely and cheat themselves out of wonderful friendships is that they truly don't know the basics of being friendly. It is really quite simple: be *others*-centered.

Even before you show up, think consciously about the questions you may ask in order to give that friend an opportunity to be heard and understood. (Isn't that what we all want?) You may have to flip through your mental file folder on that person's recent history and determine exactly how to let her know you are not just mindful of but are *interested in* her life situation. You may ask questions such as:

- "How is work going? Did you end up getting that raise?"

- "How is your husband's back? Was he able to schedule a surgery?"

- "How are things coming on your house addition? Are you finding it hard to juggle everything else along with that?"

One question I like to ask in the context of whatever challenge that person is facing is, "Are you feeling encouraged lately?"

If it's been a while or if you don't know the person very well, start small, but start!

- "How's life treating you?"

- "What does your typical day look like?"

- "What would be the most helpful thing for you right now?" (Make suggestions. Prime the pump! She's not likely to admit, "I'd love a casserole and a sitter some evening.")

- "How do your kids like school?"

- "What do you like to do for fun?"

There is nothing like a one-way conversation to kill a potential friendship or weaken the bonds of an existing one. The person who can talk of nothing other than herself and her problems will remain a social shut-in. When we sit down with someone, we should assume they could very well be getting ready to jump off the proverbial bridge, *no matter how Prada-good they look on the outside*. Take a risk and tenderly ask questions such as, "Are you and your family doing OK with...?" It is better to err on the side of caring too much than not caring enough.

Secondly, don't assume the responsibility of "fixing" the person's problem. Resist the urge to offer platitudes and quote Scripture. And don't try to compare her problem to yours. "I understand what you mean about a tight budget. We had to cancel our Disney vacation this year."

The best kind of friend comforts with her eyes and ears. One of the greatest gifts you can give to a friend is a voice. Let her be heard. Allow your quiet, gentle presence to do what words may fail to do. Do you remember the Old Testament story of Job? He'd lost everything— his family, his possessions, his health, and his livelihood. Upon hearing Job's tragic news, his friends came over to comfort him.

They did well for seven days—just sat there in silence with Job, all dirty and unshaven. Then one of them opened his mouth, and the rest chimed in, trying to "help." That is why the Book of Job is over forty chapters long, and that is why time spent with certain friends of yours may feel just as long. If your heart is focused more on loving than advising, you will know when it is the right time to speak.

The God Who Dries Our Tears

Nothing anyone could say would touch the pain I felt when I lost my first baby. He was gone before I could hold him in my arms. Jason and I named him Luke, and we began the process of healing.

A few weeks later I started feeling ill. I thought I had a stomach bug. When I didn't get better, I wondered, "Could I be pregnant?" I found myself again in my bathroom, staring at two pink vertical lines, tears running down my cheeks. Only this time I was not overjoyed; I was terrified. How could this happen? How could I accept and rejoice over this pregnancy when I was still mourning the loss of Luke? What if something went wrong? I didn't want to be pregnant again. Not this soon. Maybe never.

The next week I was able to get away alone for a while. During a quiet time I felt God speaking to my heart. "Don't you know how much I love you? Don't you know that when your heart was breaking, Mine was breaking too?"

All I could answer was, "I didn't know, Lord. Please forgive me." I cried for a long time, feeling all the grief pouring out of me. When I was finished, I reached up to wipe my eyes, but they were dry. The Lord spoke to me again: "I will wipe every tear from your eyes." (See Revelation 21:4.)

I could hardly believe it. For the first time in weeks the inner pain was gone. I no longer felt empty. God had healed my broken heart. I reached down, placed my hand on my belly, and said, "I love you, little one, and I want you."

Today I have a beautiful, precious little boy named Noah. He is an unexpected gift, one I cannot imagine life without. Of course I miss Luke, but I know that he is in a beautiful place, safe with our Savior, and one day I will hold him in my arms too.

—JULIE HARMON

Places to Find Friendship: MOPS and Other Life Boats

Moms' groups are excellent places to form enduring friendships. I got involved in MOPS (Mothers of Preschoolers International) while pregnant with Anna and remained active in the group for over a decade.[3] Twice a month I'd deposit my girls into the hands of sweet, elderly ladies who made crafts with them while I found solace in the company of other women who smelled like spit-up and had bed hair. It was a sort of an "AA-for-moms" meeting.

I didn't always feel like waking up early to get to the meetings, though. Sometimes the speakers were dull or addressing topics I wasn't concerned about. One time a police officer was going to tell us about child car seat safety. Who in a group of thirty young moms wouldn't know about that? I slammed the snooze button ten times before finally rolling out of bed, deciding that maybe MOPS wasn't all about *me*. Maybe I could encourage someone there that day.

The policewoman brought her K-9, who sat beside her while she droned on about the proper positioning of infants in a car seat. It was as boring as the smell in the room was bad. A foul odor caused every mom holding a baby to lift him in the air and sniff his diaper while the officer was talking. No one could identify the culprit. At the end of her presentation the policewoman said, "Please excuse Hoover's flatulence. I changed his dog food, and it's not agreeing with him."

But two things made sitting in that fetid air well worth it: First, the lady offered us all brand new car seats through a safety program the local police force was sponsoring. I would need one, as I was pregnant with Sarah. Secondly, and more importantly, God had sent me there for "Marcie." Marcie was a fellow mom who also had reason not to show up that day: her husband had just lost his job, and she was feeling down. I found this out by locking eyes with her and asking, "How are you?" and really meaning it, actually waiting for an answer. I was able to hear her out and offer just enough hope-filled words to lift her spirits.

Of course MOPS isn't the only place to meet other moms. There are parent resource centers, play groups, and general moms groups not linked to any larger organization. If no such thing exists in your area, maybe it's time to start one yourself. I guarantee you, you're not alone in wishing there was such a place. Friendship and encouragement are yours for the finding!

Why Moms Should Go to Church

I remember once complaining to my friend Diane about being confined to a nursery for the duration of every Sunday morning church service—actually for the duration of my kids' early childhood years. "What's the point in going to church?" I asked her.

She said, "Faith, it might be that MOPS is going to be your 'church' for a while." Her words proved true. A woman is not going to get much inspiration from rocking near a Diaper Genie in a church nursing room. However, I continued to drag myself to church, convinced of the following reasons for not jumping ship too soon:

- My kids wouldn't always be little. They *would* stop drawing on the tithing envelopes and dawdling near the baptismal some day. No, one day they would be *in* the baptismal.

- Church is a good place to find future spouses for your children. Keep a watch for that two-year-old who picks his socks up off the floor.

- There's something powerful about corporate worship—a diverse crowd of people with similar struggles, all cheering for the same God.

- Sometimes the pastor will preach something you find to be applicable to your personal life. If not, God will speak through someone else.

Keep your ears open in the ladies' room or at the diaper-changing station.

- Church is an opportunity to get all dressed up and have a place to go. This is good for our mental health.

- There will likely be at least one other person there who understands you. If not, there will certainly be one person who needs to be understood.

- Churches provide opportunities for mothers to use their talents. People shouldn't be limited to singing in the shower! (Well, some should.)

- Being at church gives you a chance to teach your child to sit still for long periods of time. Very long periods of time.

- Church is not about the four walls; the church is *people*. You just might meet a kindred spirit there.

- Finally (drum roll please), the church (all believers) is *the only physical representation of Jesus Christ on the earth today*. Why wouldn't we want to gather on a regular basis in the places where "the body of Christ" is found in highest concentration?

There is something mystical that happens when we assemble with people "in the same boat," with the same Captain: we come away from such experiences feeling spiritually empowered and recharged—and this can even happen from behind the tinted windows of a nursery. "Let us not give up meeting together, as some are in the habit of doing" (Heb. 10:25).

If you don't belong to a church and would like to know how to find a good one, I'll give you a few tips. Look for a church that:

- Keeps the person of Jesus Christ at the center of the teachings

- Uses the Bible as the source of the teachings

- Isn't exclusive. If they project the idea that belonging to their particular fellowship is the only "true church," get out!

My list may be surprisingly short. If I make it longer, it will only create undue expectations and turn out more church hoppers than church shoppers. Find a good church and *be* the change you want to see there. Be the friendly face, the welcoming handshake for a visitor. Be a voice for the overlooked and a place setting for the lonely. Ask to teach a class on domestic violence or raise awareness about human trafficking. Bring what you have to offer.

Social Networking

I can't close this discussion on loneliness without addressing one of the most common ways we seek to cure it—online social networking. Are you guilty, as I am, of abusing this technology?

I spend my days parked under a laptop in a remote

log cabin. And I probably have a touch of ADD, hence my excuses for pausing every now and then (read: more times than I care to admit) to browse the news feed. If all Facebook friends stuck with weather and dinner reports, the latest occurrence of stomach flu in the family and so on, I'd be OK. But people have to go and post the most interesting stuff! There are babies and travels and book deals and blog posts and events and news articles and someone is no longer single! I want to be in the know.

I want to be *connected*. And I don't apologize for *that*; it's how God made us.

If you're as active on Facebook as I am, I don't have to list for you the advantages of having an account and using it. (You may be reading this book because of Facebook. I don't know if that helps my case or not.) But the other side of the truth is, *Facebook is a robber.* It robs us of productivity and steals time with our families and sometimes with God.

I have attempted to correct this problem in my life by several means: I've waited until my bladder was about to burst before opening Facebook so I'd be forced to zip through posts quickly. I'm famous for deactivating my account over and over. My children suggested I watch a Netflix documentary called *Facebook Obsession*. (I will.) Recently I exercised "Parental Control" by creating a "Faith Child" user account on my computer and blocking the website. My friends laugh at me, and I wonder if I'm the only one who enjoys connecting this much with people I'll otherwise never see.

While I am humbly "confessing my sin" to you, I am also acknowledging three things:

1. We were made for relationship.

2. We need to be transparent in our relation-ships. (Don't you feel better, fellow addict? My name is Face Bogdan, and I am a Faithbookaholic. Hic!)

3. We need a higher power—that is, the Highest Power.

Which brings me to the most important part of this book...

 Refrigerator Magnet: God is ever present through each lonely day of this short season.

 Heart Exam: What are the personal issues that keep me from reaching out for friendship?

Chapter 14

THREE BRAVE AND BEAUTIFUL WORDS

T HE OTHER DAY a friend dropped by the house and sat with me on the front porch for a while. The two of us sipped hot tea and wrapped ourselves in blankets to keep out a cold March wind. She'd come to give voice to an inner struggle over a life-altering decision. During the course of our conversation my friend said three of the most brave and beautiful words a human being can string together: "I need God."

If you go to the top of the stairs of my log cabin and turn right, down the hall you'll come to a large master bedroom with a knotty pine cathedral ceiling and giant support beams stretched across the room. On the nightstand rests a weathered Bible with pages hanging from threads, a set of earplugs, and a box of tissues—testaments to a felt need for God. Each morning before my feet hit the floor, I take some time to check in with the One who enlisted me in this service called motherhood.

I'm not much for religion per se (I'll explain why soon), but I'm all about getting to know Jesus. He is love incarnate, the physical expression of God. His indwelling Spirit is everything a human needs to be properly human and all a mother needs to succeed in raising kids. He is provision, protection, acceptance, affirmation, understanding, compassion, patience, grace. God is not surprised by our failures or disappointed in us as moms.

Thankfully He doesn't act as we do sometimes with our kids—moaning and groaning about having to constantly clean up our messes, redirect us, and steer us clear of trouble. He's not drumming His fingers on the judgment seat, rolling His eyes at our childish behavior, impatiently tapping the floor with His foot as we flounder through life. He already knew about the temper thing; He wasn't shocked when you raised your voice yesterday.

God longs to help us, to roll in like a cleansing rain in the middle of our deserts. He dreams of what we could be—even has the blueprint—if we'd be willing to walk away from the construction site that is our life and let Him take over—lay ourselves wide open for a heart transplant; give Him the helm long before the iceberg comes into view; finally open the letter, return the call, show up, and see what happens. But Jesus is a gentleman. He doesn't force Himself on anyone.

Sometimes you have to forget what you've heard or wrongly believed about God and give Him a chance to speak for Himself. Raise the white flag, be brave and strong enough to leave pride by the side of the road and become a weakling before God. Rip off the fig leaves and let Him see it all. Confess to your craving for intimacy with someone who places no condition on us except that we return His love in the form of reckless surrender and total abandonment of ourselves in worship.

This is what humans want, and this is what humans do. We all worship *something*.

Call it conversion to Christianity, or call it what you will, but make no mistake—reconciliation with the Creator does not mean reciting a creed, filling out a card, going to church, keeping the rules, joining a do-gooders' club, or becoming a straight-laced prude. The first step in becoming a follower of Christ is confessing to Him in no uncertain terms that you are ultimately an absolute failure of a person on your own. (This will be no shock to God.) If you're not sure whether that's true of you, if you're one of those who insist we humans are inherently good, you haven't met a two-year-old. Or maybe you reason that the tantrum-throwing child has simply forgotten he is good. You'd be right in a sense.

We, dear mothers, *were* at one time good. Perfect, in fact. We were naked and flawless before God and man—without a single gray hair, stretch mark, or cellulite dimple. Soothing and nurturing words filled our lips at all times, our hearts pumped only thoughts of peace, and self-abandoning love coursed through our veins. Never a single insecure notion entered our innocent minds.

But one day a silly idea occurred—a ridiculous string of thoughts hung suspended before Eve's eyes, and she lingered, considering: "I don't need God's help. I can do this on my own. I *am* all that!"

The last part was true; we *were* like God in a sense—His spittin' image in the way we behaved and carried ourselves. My friend Lou once told me that all Eve had to say to the deceiver was, "I already *am like God*. Get over it." And all the while she'd have known and we'd always remember that we can be like Him only *with His help*. But that's not exactly what the snake had in mind.

Eve took that empowering bite of knowledge, and pride entered, like a cancer cell, spreading to the human race and killing our dependence on God. Fig leaves of shame and guilt covered Eve's once-confident soul. Intimacy was lost.

God cried and pursued and said, "Where are you?" (though He well knew). "Where is the woman I made? I want to see *her* again. The *world* needs to see her. She needs to see herself, *find her true self again.*" But Eve forgot who she was—and whose she was.

Like spiritual two-year-olds we have forgotten we were made to be *good* and *He* is *good.* We have forgotten because the knowledge of good and evil—that first disastrous yielding—made our hearts sick and had a toxic bearing on our minds and won't leave us alone night and day. Thrown into utter confusion, we now doubt ourselves and doubt the One who made us. Or else we parade ourselves as goddesses, thinking we can be all and do all, never minding that we have no idea why we are here and what life really means.

And while it has become popular to question the reality of good and evil, how often does our speech betray our heart beliefs, hour by hour, in words that speak of good and bad as we long to see wrongs made right? We want to see wrongs made right because the One who made us loves justice. We take after God in our desire to see this world made right—a new earth with its inhabitants redeemed and restored to the place where every created thing lives in the freedom of Eden—a world where plants breathe clean air and fish swim in pure water and humans don't waste words or pollute the atmosphere with hateful speech.

We create and fix things, being made in the image of the Creator and Healer, but we can do only so much. After all—we are just the image. So God came clothed in our skin, named Himself Jesus, and said, "This is what I meant." He showed us how to be properly human— breathing in and living out of the divine nature—fully mature fruit of a human mother's womb—a mother like you and me. Mary was descended from Eve, but instead of attempting to be like God *without God*, she chose rather to say, "How will this be?" (Luke 1:34). How on earth am I to do this—raise God's child?

I need help. I need God.

God helped her as He helps me and wants to help us all, and Mary grew that crying baby into a boy—a boy who also recognized His utter dependence on God and tried hard at twelve to tell the religious folks that being about the Father's business of people-restoration is the only thing worth living for.

But they were more interested in the preservation of self and tired traditions, and those are two enemies of God-reliance: humanism and religion. They both deny the need for help from a higher power outside of oneself. *Religious* people rely on the rituals *they themselves* have made in order to appease God, when all He wants is Adam and Eve back—you and me—transparent and unashamed, living in the joyous abandon of intimacy with God.

Jesus was "all that." He was called "the second Man or Last Adam" (1 Cor. 15:45, 47). And some saw His example and wanted to be like Him—as I so desperately do—but

He is holy. Perfectly holy. And we, after the garden, were none of that anymore.

But the holy and just One desired us nonetheless, and what's a holy God to do when the object of His affection is too sin-stained to abide in His presence? He finds a way to bridge the divide, to break down the wall keeping us apart. Then He writes centuries of love letters bound in a book, containing one urgent message: *Meet Me at the cross.*

One day I followed Jesus's trail of tears and blood and found Him hanging there, wearing every guilt-garment of mine He could find, letting me know it was over—this using my shame as an excuse to hide, this endless running on pathetic self-confidence. He'd let the haters beat Him, and I'll never forget His eyes on me as they did: *I'll see you on the other side,* they promised.

And He did. He showed up dressed for a wedding, scars peeking beneath the cuffs, and how could I keep running? How can we run from a lover who promises, "I will make you my wife forever, showing you righteousness and justice, unfailing love and compassion" (Hosea 2:19, NLT)?

Missing the Mark

People who have the "misfortune" of an easy and prosperous life, or who make knowledge their higher power, are among those who may never come to realize their need for a Savior. That is the greatest of human tragedies. Mercifully I was able to recognize that I am not the whole being I was created to be. Sin was the great divide that kept me in a desperate, alone condition apart from God—whether I'd realize it here or hereafter.

People tend to think only of immoral acts and dirty habits when they hear the word *sin*. But the meaning of the word in the original text—the New Testament Greek definition—is simply "missing the mark."[1] God had a bull's-eye—a "perfect self" in mind for each of us. Anything we become or do that's the slightest bit "off the mark" is sin.

So I sin when I am afraid. Insecure. Paranoid. Untrusting. Assuming. Presuming. Irritated. Bitter. High-minded. Nosey and gossipy or withdrawn and detached. I sin by being stingy and by overspending. Starving myself or being a glutton. Withholding affection. Running from reality. Being insensitive or too sensitive. Doubt, cynicism, greed, waste, laziness, obsession, and procrastination—these are sins. Every time I act, speak, or think in a way not in line with God's intent for my life, I sin. And He is saddened because He knows who I am supposed to be and how much more at peace and productive—spiritually *re*productive—I would be if I were free to be that person.

Conversion involves seeing sin for what it is and owning it honestly before God. Repentance follows, which means making a 180-degree turn, at least in mind and heart. Spiritual growth resulting in changed behavior is a lifelong process that begins with inviting God's Spirit to live within. As you feed this God-living-in-you revelation through meditating in the Scriptures—as if soaking a seed—and through prayer and surrounding yourself with people of like faith, the change will become more and more evident. (We discussed this in chapter 4.) Jesus called this "bearing spiritual fruit" (John 15).

But again, being a Christian is more than changing for the better; that's just the by-product of relationship. It's about being close to God.

It's often during the darkest times, as I rest in silence, that I feel His presence surround me. The pure essence of who God is—love—sometimes engulfs me in a way that makes me hardly able to leave the floor where I pray. I lie there for a while, enjoying what we were all meant to enjoy—the presence of my Creator and closest friend. When I get up, I feel renewed and ready to face my world again—an empowered and well-loved woman, certain I can go where no one has gone before.

A Love I Couldn't Resist

I learned to hate early on. I was abandoned by my mother at age three, physically and verbally abused by my stepmother, and sexually molested by her son throughout my childhood. It all left me emotionally paralyzed to genuine acts of love.

There was one act of love I couldn't resist though: Jesus's death for me. When I learned of it, I knew it was all I needed. I desperately wanted to be filled with that kind of love. The transformation from hating to loving was both instantaneous and the beginning of a lifelong process.

It began as I cradled my newborn in my arms. I was overwhelmed by the knowledge that I had never known how to love and that I'd been given a brief window of opportunity (about eighteen years) to get it right. I had to start immediately. But how? All I'd ever known was abuse and hate.

My son Nathan was a happy but strong-willed child. As he challenged my authority, I had flashbacks. I remembered what terrible things had happened to me when I did nothing wrong, let alone challenged my stepmother. I was determined not to continue the pattern of abuse. Frustration with Nathan's behavior bottled up inside me. My only recourse was to run to my room and cry, "God, help! I need You!"

Those were desperate yet precious times. As God rushed to my side in those moments, I realized His unconditional love for both Nathan and me. I learned how to love and be loved. As God continues to teach me how to love with *His* kind of love, I realize that what I want my children to remember most about me is that I love them, I love their daddy, and I love the God who made this all possible.

—Robin Ogg

The Most Powerful Force

It has been said that love is the most powerful force in the universe. People of all faiths and walks of life understand this. If we could love and be loved unconditionally, we'd all be OK, and the world wouldn't be broken as it is. But what we fail to understand is that we are incapable of this kind of love. We may think we have a grasp on it—until someone misjudges, disrespects, humiliates, ignores, or rejects us; questions our motives; fails to tolerate us; takes advantage of us; breaks the favorite vase— or breaks the heart. Suddenly it's not so easy to love without condition.

The apostle Paul, when writing to the Corinthians, said that one can be completely charitable—giving away all her possessions and fighting for worthy causes—but not have a clue as to what true love means (1 Cor. 13). True love means you don't even *think* negatively about someone. You don't react. You can suffer unkindness for a long time and still be kind in the suffering. You believe the best about people and don't feel smug when someone who rubs you the wrong way falls on her face. You never envy or try to promote yourself. There's more, but that alone is a tall order.

And when you apply it to feeling God's unconditional love for you, it's even more difficult. The humanists like to say we need only to look inside ourselves to be loved and accepted. Come on, how unconditionally do you really love yourself? I know how I feel about myself after I've yelled at one of my kids and sent her to her room crying. Or when I've been tempted to scream, *"I'm sick of kids!"*

I remember how I felt about myself as a newlywed. I was young, insecure, and immature. I cried pretty much the whole first year of marriage. I was convinced all Dave could see of me was my faults—the way I couldn't cook, hated mornings, didn't have the right figure and muscle tone, and was hypersensitive, which only magnified all my weaknesses and perceived disapproval by my husband. If he looked at me cross-eyed, I'd fall apart, sure I hadn't measured up.

The first day he came home from work after we were married, it was a couple hours earlier than I'd expected. I was wearing a threadbare T-shirt and pair of holey sweatpants, scrubbing the bathtub on all fours with a ponytail shooting geyser-like from the top of my head. I was sweaty and stinky. That's how Dave found his bride when he walked in the door.

I threw a fit over him not warning me he'd be early so I could at least get freshened up. Dinner was far from ready. As I stood there blithering about my sorry state, a look I'll never forget came across his face—a mixture of sadness and amusement. I couldn't tell if he was going to burst out laughing or turn around and leave.

"What is it?" I demanded, wiping a dusting of scouring powder from my face.

"Can I just get a kiss from my beautiful wife?" he said.

I fell into his arms and cried like a baby.

For the next year David Bogdan loved me through more tearful and hormonal episodes, and he has continued to love me for the past nineteen years. It was his unconditional love that helped grow me into the wife he needed. And it is God's love—infinitely more powerful than that of the best husband on earth—that grows us into the people He needs to change the world.

The point of changing the world is that we are eternal, spiritual beings whom God wants by His side *forever*—to experience the eternal, fullest enjoyment of relationship with God and with others. When a mother points her child's heart toward heaven, she may be pointing countless others—maybe even millions—there as well.

So on to it! Here's to knowing Him (or knowing Him better) and leading little ones to such a knowledge. There's not much time. In fact, the only time we have is *now.* Let's conclude this book on that thought as we proceed to the final chapter.

Refrigerator Magnet: The best way to find my true self is to get to know my Maker.

 Heart Exam: Am I more of a "good person"—or an imperfect person being made whole through an authentic relationship with Jesus?

Chapter 15

"WANDER WOMAN"—
LIVING IN THE PRESENT

HOW MUCH MARKETING are you expected to do?" I asked the author as she signed my copy of her new book. We were conversing, writer to writer, about the ins and outs of book publishing. This young, brilliant mother was where I wanted to be in life—or so I thought.

"Oh, publishing companies really want you to help with promotion. I do TV, radio, book signings, and appearances," she smiled as she autographed another book.

My heart sank. "Does it take you away from your family very much?"

"It doesn't have to, if you budget your time well."

Easier said than done. I thanked the celebrity mom and walked away, my emotions torn. I wanted to be able to sit where she was, and yet I didn't feel quite ready to embrace the turn my life could take as a published writer.

Granted, this is my first book, and I am fully aware that this humble endeavor may end up on aisle seven at the Dollar Tree. But what if it does sell more than a few copies? Am I ready to abandon the cruise control of my life and enter the fast lane populated by authors and such?

In the days following the author encounter, I wavered

between wanting to hole away and complete my book and almost ditching the project altogether. The reason for my uncertainty? I have fallen hopelessly in love with my children. I want to be with them. I want to make beaded jewelry in the evenings with them and fly kites on windy days. I want to read a few more Shel Silverstein rhymes in the green chair while three can still fit and snuggle with them under warm blankets on wintry mornings, listening to outrageous dreams of the night before.

I want to make at least a dozen more trips to Roaring Run Creek and listen to squeals of delight as crawfish plop into buckets and minnows nibble tiny toes. I want to chase wayward tennis balls until my sides hurt, before the young lady who used to be my baby finds another partner on some faraway campus. I want to feel the crushing weight of heavy teenaged frames on my lap as many more times as they'll let me.

I am afraid. I am afraid that in becoming "Author-Mom" I might miss something. I may come home from a book signing one evening and find Anna engaged to be married or Sarah up and gone to journalism school. I may return to find that Ruthie doesn't slurp in her sleep as she sucks her thumb to a white prune anymore, and that Rebecca no longer needs to nestle beside me in the cushy chair and let me help her through a long-division problem.

As I tore myself away from a disastrous kitchen to go write this morning, there was a lump in my throat. I wanted to stay home. My heart was embracing the mess of strawberry hulls and sticky red juice that covered the table and hair that begged to be brushed. My arms were desperate to tighten around Rebecca and never let go as she beamed, "Now don't be gone long!" A big part of me considered not leaving at all—laying down this book project and not picking it up again until there are no more little girls in the house to draw my heart back home.

But I must tell my story now, to the multitude of kid-weary moms who trudge through endless days of thankless labor. I am here to say that time and love change the job. It does become easier. High chairs, Pampers, and potty seats are but artifacts of a distant past. In my mind I can still smell the salty-sweetness of a newborn scalp, though. How I wish I'd rocked and held them longer.

Many times I didn't rock and hold at all. There was simply too much to do. That is the part that doesn't change. There is *always* too much to do. I am in danger of "getting stuff done," only to wake up one morning and find some things missing: that sweaty smell of Sarah's hair after she's come in from catching critters in our little pond, the sight of "scum-sock" on her legs from going shin deep in algae water to capture one more salamander. I will not wish I'd spent more time wiping smudged windows and cleaning out cupboards. I will wish I'd paid as much mind to catastrophic bedrooms as I do a gnat in the farmer's field down the road.

Getting "Radical"

In his book *Radical: Taking Back Your Faith From the American Dream* David Platt talks about Jesus's prayer as He's nearing the end of His life on earth. Jesus tells the Father, "I have finished the work You gave me to do here." Then He goes on to summarize that work (John 17).

Now, Jesus could have said, "I led a massive health care

reform by healing the sick, fed thousands with very little resources, and revolutionized the way people think about women, children, and minority groups. I turned the religious institution on its head and defined social justice. I inaugurated a kingdom that will divide history in half and demonstrated the way to live successfully human. Oh, and I raised the dead."

At least that's how *I* would have summarized my accomplishments if I were Jesus. But what did He actually say? "I took care of the twelve guys You gave Me."

As Platt puts it, Jesus "staked everything on His relationships with twelve men.... [They] were the small group responsible for carrying on all that Jesus had begun."[1]

In other words, Jesus was focused. I wonder if that's what it really means to be "radical"—to invest in the right things and people instead of being all over the place physically or mentally, getting a lot of things done and thought through while ignoring the very thing I am meant to do and think about today, the thing with which I can most impact the world.

Where would Christianity be if Jesus had not focused *most of His time* on twelve young, ordinary men? It was they who "turned the world upside down" (Acts 17:6, NKJV). Up until then there was nothing immediately gratifying about training fishermen with tempers and thick skulls. There was no employer review, paycheck, or mountain of feedback for all Jesus endured with those guys—losing sleep, facing storms at sea, going without hot meals, breaking up immature quarrels, and snuffing out little fires of religious zeal.

Yet at the end of a day of miracles, it was this circle of

ragtag men with whom Jesus sailed away from His crowd of admirers. They were the ones seated around the breakfast fire on the beach, learning that life is about feeding sheep. They were the ones getting their feet washed by God in a dimly lit room with only the sound of dirty water dripping from His hands.

I have my own little group of disciples. Their names are Anna, Sarah, Rebecca, and Ruthie. What if I am to change the world through one or all of them? What if, while I sit here daydreaming, a bonfire turns to dying embers—the very one I'm supposed to gather around with these few to teach them how to feed more sheep? What if those small feet outgrow the opportunity for washing while I strive for lesser opportunities amid the ring of applause? Aren't these precious few the ones I should invest in if I want to radically change the world?

Slow Dancing in the Dark

Dirty dishes. Sticky floors. Unpacked lunches. Piled laundry. The "yet-to-do" list at 9:00 p.m. was long. All five children were *finally* tucked in bed, with visions of healthy lunches and clean underwear awaiting them in the morning (well, those were *my* visions, anyway). Goodnight kisses were given and final questions answered. Even the turbo-charged toddler was asleep. My weary body longed for Calgon, but nobody was going to take me away tonight. I had chores to do.

I was barely down the stairs when screams of "I neeeeed you!" came from the toddler's room.

"Need me? You won't want me if I come in there!" I snarled inwardly. The last thing I wanted to be was "needed." I continued whining to myself as my attitude plummeted from a "needs improvement" rating to "needs intervention."

The bedroom continued to emit shrieks, and I dragged myself back up the stairs. My impulse was to add to the shrieks, but by some miracle self-control showed up and I squeaked out, "What's wrong, baby?"

The tiny voice from the crib whispered, "I don't know. I just need you."

Dishes took a backseat suddenly and with curious ease. The soft praise music I had turned on in my son's room enveloped us as we began to rock.

His tears stopped. Mine started. How would I learn to savor eternal moments without the health commission condemning my home?

"Mommy, will you dance with me?" came the tender request.

Dance we did. Just me and my baby, slow dancing in the darkness.

He went to bed peacefully, and so did I. Dishes undone, lunches unpacked. By God's grace I would learn to savor eternal moments, one interruption at a time.

—LAURA RIZKALLAH

"Mom!"

In his book *The Shack* Paul Young points out that we spend most of our time, not in the present, but in the past or future. This is tragic. And, sadly, it is *the thing* that causes me to lose my cool with my kids or ignore them sometimes. It is why I have earned the nickname "Wander Woman." Too often my mind wanders to an imperfect past or to the immediate and distant future. I'm thinking about what's for dinner, what the insensitive friend said to offend me, or how we'll pay the bills, and somewhere a frustrated Ruthie is calling, "Mom! Mom! *Mom!*"

It's a rotten business, entertaining everything but the present. It makes me a very bad mother sometimes.

Learning to live in the present is beautifully illustrated in the movie *Peaceful Warrior*, which is based on a true story. Gymnast Dan Millman is consumed with the future, "the destination"—getting the Olympic gold. Thinking it will bring him happiness, he ignores where true happiness is found: on the journey. It's not until he surrenders control over the future and embraces—pays attention to, appreciates—the present that he finds real peace and joy. I love the film's ending. Dan is suspended, high in the air on the still rings, toes pointed, concentrating before a hushed arena. A still, small voice questions, "Where are you, Dan?"

He answers, "Here."

"What time is it?"

"Now."

"What are you?"

"This moment."

With that, Dan goes into the grand finale of his gymnastic routine and does what his coach says "no one on the planet can do." He flips and flips and flips between the rings with grace and ease, and then dismounts.

Being Present

My cousin Autumn is a type B personality, which I've concluded must stand for "Box." The reason she can fall asleep in any location, on any surface, and in any position is because there is a box in her brain into which she climbs and can shut out every distracting thought and fall asleep in a nanosecond. When she told me that, I thought how nice it would be to have such a box in my brain, because when my head hits the pillow at night, it doesn't slow down but keeps right on thinking about all the things mothers think about. I decided to see if by chance I may have been endowed with an "Autumn Box" and not known it all these years.

I climbed into bed, lay on my back, and embedded my head in my pillow like a spoon in mashed potatoes. I slapped my lavender-scented flaxseed-filled sleeping mask across my eyes, eager to find my long-lost box. My jaws dropped open and I waited, relaxed like a corpse. Sure enough, there it was, my very own compartmentalizing box, big enough for me to crawl into and fall asleep as fast as my cousin does. I mentally squeezed into it, assumed the fetal position, and closed the flaps. Within seconds a tragic realization hit me—my box is see-through!

Autumn-with-a-Box came to visit me with her four small children one day. She stepped out of her minivan, and I noticed one of her feet was decidedly orange. *Orange.* I wondered if she'd eaten too many carrots (she's a juicer) and was suffering from an overdose of beta-carotene, or if she'd done a pedicure with henna. I had to ask.

"Oh, my kids did that. I allow them to color on my feet with markers while I take a nap. They love it."

I felt a twinge of guilt mixed with envy. Here was "Wonder Woman." She was the real deal. She knew how to live in the present.

An hour later Autumn reclined in my La-Z-Boy, her other foot transformed into a canvas. Our young Picassos had the time of their lives giving her an artisan pedicure.

Of course my kids wondered when *"Wander* Woman" was going to let them do the same to her...

The next time they ask, I hope to be paying attention. As I lie there, feeling the tickle of Crayola washables on my heels and listening to giggles over toes-turned-little-people, I may hear a voice whisper, "Where are you, Faith?"

I hope I'll answer, "Here."

 Refrigerator Magnet: Today I will live each moment in the present.

 Heart Exam: Where has my mind been focused the most lately? Can I surrender this part of my life to God?

Acknowledgments

To Sarah—do you remember the day we sat in the car by the river and listened to the call of sea gulls as I read to you every word I'd written about you in the pages of this book? Mother and daughter cried together as I said words you so needed to hear. Hearts were mended, and we drove away with an energized love for each other. That was a new beginning in our relationship, Sarah, and I thank you for being gracious enough to let me share our story in hopes that other Sarahs and moms of Sarahs will be encouraged—even healed by it. You are—in spite of me—becoming a lady of extravagant grace, tender compassion, and keen insight into the nature of things. I am extremely proud of you.

To Anna—thank you for holding down the fort while I wrote this book; for stepping in to help with the cooking (and for loving it) and for baking batches of cookies to feed a starving artist and looking the other way as I snatched yet another from the cooling pan. I appreciate your understanding and patient waiting for me to reenter society after completing this book. Space would fail me to tell of your total awesomeness; you, dear teenager, rock.

To Rebecca—thank you for being such a wonderful big sister to Ruthie, for patiently climbing down from your bunk in the night to accompany her to the bathroom without ever waking me up. Thank you for delivering endless mugs of reheated coffee to me without complaint and for enduring every smothering kiss on your very kissable cheeks. You are mature beyond your years. If I had a ten-year-old, I'd want her to be just like you.

To Ruthie—Ruthie, are you there? I'm talking to you! I know you now know everything there is to know and are ready to hit the runway, but before you do, I'd like to take a moment to thank you for coming into my life. You have filled it with immeasurable joy. I can't wait to see what you become when you grow up—tomorrow. Always remember the little people, including your mother.

To Dave—thank you for being proud of me. It means more than any accolade. You are simply the best husband a woman could ever ask for and the best daddy-prince I could ever want for our four princesses. I still don't understand why God saw fit to give me you, but I'm no less grateful than I was the day I said, "I do," and still humbled by the gift of your companionship and devotion. Thank you above all for putting God first and thus helping me be more of what He intended.

To Mom and Dad—I'm thankful mostly for two things: you modeled what good parenting is and who the best Parent of all is. Thank you for pointing me to the Father's heart early on and every day for as long as you had me. Anything wise in this book comes, ultimately, as a result of your hearts. Dad, thank you for taking time (eight hours straight!) out of your busy schedule to read and critique the manuscript. Yours and Mom's encouragement meant the world to me at a time when I felt like giving up.

To friends who read the manuscript—each one of you is a busy mom like me, yet you gave me the gift of your time and enthusiasm, which encouraged me to go on. You all became my cheerleading squad and gave me assurance that I was on the right track. Your feedback proved invaluable. Sharon Evans, my brilliant aunt—your speedy, heartfelt, and expert review was the boost I needed.

To my story contributors—thank you for so honestly and openly sharing your stories with us. In moments of self-doubt you reminded me that I'm not alone and that there are many more moms, just like us, who need this book. Thank you for taking the time to add your beautiful voices to these pages.

To the team at Charisma House—thank you for taking a risk on a newbie like me. I grew up reading *Charisma* magazine (almost right down the road from you!), and to think of myself as one of your authors is such an honor. Thank you for your superb work on every aspect of this book. Adrienne Gaines, I appreciate your organizational expertise and sharp eye for detail, not to mention your kind spirit.

To God, "Daddy"—How well I recall that predawn morning after signing this book contract when I sat wrapped in a blanket like Mary, looking up at the stars and asking if You really thought I could do this. I'll never forget You answering me with Gabriel's words: "Rejoice...the Lord is with you....Do not be afraid...for you have found favor with God....The Holy Spirit will come upon you, and the power of the Highest will overshadow you" (Luke 1:28, 30, 35, NKJV).

I responded to Your voice by softly singing "Spirit of the living God, fall afresh on me," and instantly a gentle star fell across the sky—which I felt was a sign of Your promised favor. I had sat down on those porch steps scared and unsure of myself, but I rose up fully believing I could do anything You called me to do. The world thinks I wrote this book, but You and I know the truth. You did it through me. *We* did it—together. We *did* it, God! You amaze me. I can't wait to see what You do next.

Notes

Chapter 5
The Challenge Child

1. *The Secret Life of Bees*, directed by Gina Prince-Bythewood (2008; Hollywood, CA: 20th Century Fox, 2009), DVD.
2. ADHDChildParenting.com, "The Advantages of Attention Deficit Disorder," http://www.adhdchildparenting.com/the -advantages-of-add.php (accessed December 17, 2012); Pete Quily, "CIA on ADDers: 'We Need That Kind of Talent Here,'" *Adult ADD Strengths* (blog), November 25, 2006, http:// adultaddstrengths.com/2006/11/25/cia-on-adders-we-need-that -kind-of-talent-here/ (accessed December 17, 2012).

Chapter 6
Trying to Be Miss Everything

1. Bob Sorge, *Envy: The Enemy Within* (Ventura, CA: Regal Books, 2003), 17, 21.
2. Card Written by Brittany Hochstaetter, Lawson Falle Publishing, Inc., a division of Dicksons, Inc., Seymour, IN/Cambridge, Ontario, "Encouragement Moms" cards 35138C.
3. Valerie G. Lowe, "Family on the Move," *Charisma*, February 13, 2009, http://www.charismamag.com/life/family -parenting/2991-family-on-the-move?showall=&start=1 (accessed December 17, 2012).
4. Sorge, *Envy: The Enemy Within*, 92.
5. Marvin Olasky, "Newsmakers Interview: Ann Voskcamp," Newsmakers Interview Series, Patrick Henry College, viewed at http://www.youtube.com/watch?v=BizOQz4Zqyg (accessed December 17, 2012).

Chapter 8
Who's at the Center of Your Home?

1. Gary Ezzo and Robert Buckman, *On Becoming Baby Wise* (Mt. Pleasant, SC: Parent-Wise Solutions Inc., 1995, 1998, 2001), 201–204.

2. Charlotte Kemp, "Does Giving Your Child a Bath Every Night Make Them Ill?", DailyMail.co.uk, December 2, 2010, http://www.dailymail.co.uk/femail/article-1334808/Does-giving -child-bath-night-make-ill.html (accessed December 17, 2012); Health24.com, "Bath, Shower Once a Week, Study Says," March 31, 2006, http://www.health24.com/news/Bacterial_diseases/ 1-894,35215.asp (accessed December 17, 2012).

3. For more information, visit the website of Worldwide Marriage Encounter at www.wwme.org.

4. Debbie Macomber, *One Perfect Word* (New York: Howard Books, 2012), 77–78.

Chapter 9
The Other "S" Word

1. Dictionary.com, Random House, Inc., s.v. "punish," http:// dictionary.reference.com/browse/punish?s=t (accessed December 17, 2012).

2. Merriam-Webster.com, s.v. "discipline," http://www .merriam-webster.com/dictionary/discipline (accessed December 17, 2012).

3. Josh McDowell, *How to Help Your Child Say No to Sexual Pressure* (Nashville: Word Books, 1987), 44.

4. Laura Thatcher Ulrich, *Well-Behaved Women Seldom Make History* (New York: Vintage Books, 2008).

Chapter 10
Tailor-Made Discipline

1. Gary Chapman, *The 5 Love Languages* (Chicago: Northfield Publishing, 2010).

2. Lisa Whelchel, *Creative Correction* (Carol Stream, IL: Tyndale House, 2005).

3. Kevin Leman, *Have a New Kid by Friday* (Grand Rapids, MI: Revell, 2008).

Chapter 11
Family Devotions—Eliminating the Yawn Factor

1. Dictionary.com, Random House, Inc., s.v. "devotion," http:// dictionary.reference.com/browse/devotions" (accessed December 19, 2012).

2. Ibid.

3. Christopher Peterson, "The Family Meal," *The Good Life* (blog), March 20, 2012, http://www.psychologytoday.com/blog/the-good-life/201203/the-family-meal (accessed December 19, 2012).

4. Ungame.com, "Welcome to the Official Site of the Ungame," http://www.ungame.com (accessed December 19, 2012).

5. Bruce R. Olson, *Bruchko* (Lake Mary, FL: Charisma House, 1989).

6. Hannah Hurnard, *Hinds' Feet on High Places* (Carol Stream, IL: Tyndale House Publishers, 1979).

7. Todd Burpo and Lynn Vincent, *Heaven Is for Real* (Nashville: Thomas Nelson, 2010).

8. DC Talk and the Voice of the Martyrs, *Jesus Freaks* (Tulsa, OK: Albury Publishers, 1999).

9. C. Hope Flinchbaugh, *I'll Cross the River* (Shippensburg, PA: Destiny Image, 2008).

10. Frida Gashumba, *Frida: Chosen to Die, Destined to Live* (Lancaster, England: Sovereign World, 2007).

11. C. S. Lewis, *The Chronicles of Narnia: The Lion, the Witch and the Wardrobe* (New York: HarperCollins, 2005).

Chapter 12
Just Say Yes to Fun!

1. MomsWhoThink.com, "Playdough Recipe," http://www.momswhothink.com/preschool/playdough-recipe.html (accessed December 19, 2012).

2. About.com, "Step-by-Step Slime Instructions," http://chemistry.about.com/od/chemistryactivities/ss/slimerecipe.htm (accessed December 19, 2012).

Chapter 13
I'm So Lonely!

1. "Moms and Depressions: Inside the Minds of Those Who Call for Help," *OC Family*, May 2006, http://www.ocfamily.com/t-coverstory_moms_and_depression0506.aspx (accessed December 19, 2012).

2. Carla Anne Coroy, *Married Mom, Solo Parent* (Grand Rapids, MI: Kregel Publications, 2011), 238.

3. For more information about Mothers of Preschoolers International, visit their website at www.mops.org.

Chapter 14
Three Brave and Beautiful Words

1. Biblesoft's New Exhaustive Strong's Numbers and Concordance with Expanded Greek-Hebrew Dictionary. Copyright © 1994, Biblesoft and International Bible Translators, Inc., s.v. "*hamartano*," NT:264.

Chapter 15
"Wander Woman"—Living in the Present

1. David Platt, *Radical: Taking Back Your Faith From the American Dream* (Sisters, OR: Multnomah Books, 2010), 88–89.

Recommended Resources

Discipline

Creative Correction by Lisa Welchel, Tyndale House Publishers, 2005

Have a New Kid by Friday by Dr. Kevin Leman, Revell, 2008

Making Children Mind Without Losing Yours by Dr. Kevin Leman, Revell, 2005

Marriage and family

For more on effective communication within your family, visit www.5lovelanguages.com

Marriage Encounter Weekend: for information, visit www.wwme.org

More ideas for having fun

Thriving Family magazine, a ministry of Focus on the Family

Family Fun magazine

General encouragement for moms

www.mops.org

MomSense magazine

www.hearts-at-home.org

www.proverbs31.org

EMPOWERED
TO RADICALLY CHANGE
YOUR WORLD

Charisma House brings you books, e-books, and other media from dynamic Spirit-filled Christians who are passionate about God.

Check out all of our releases from best-selling authors like **Jentezen Franklin**, **Perry Stone**, and **Joseph Prince** and experience God's supernatural power at work.

CHARISMA HOUSE

www.charismahouse.com
twitter.com/charismahouse • facebook.com/charismahouse